I Still Win

A Life of Love, Tragedy, and Triumph

Tiffany S. Greene

I Still Win: A Life of Love, Tragedy, and Triumph

ispeak
publishing company

ISpeak Publishing Service
www.ispeakpublishing.com

DEDICATION

Stephen D. Robinson Sr,

Thank you for the 23 years we shared together on this earth. All that I am today is a product of the life we shared; the ups and the downs were necessary to mold me into the woman I am today. I thank you for your love, our children, and all that you were to us! You will forever have a place in my heart. Until we meet again in Heaven, rest in peace, my love.

My boys,

Thank you, Dion, for allowing me the opportunity to write this book. With your love and support, I was able to be transparent with the truth! This book has been liberation to my soul. Thank you for understanding that our life experiences will give God glory and enable others to be healed. I love you son, with all my heart. Kedric — thank you, son, for allowing me to be a mother to you. Although you were not birthed through my womb, you have always trusted me to speak into your life and guide you in your journey. Terrance — thank you son, for understanding the struggles of a blended family, and still loving us, in spite of the circumstances. You have always been a loving and respectful young man; I love you just as if you were my own! Stephen D. Robinson Jr. — Rest in Peace, my son!

My grandfather, Willie Greene Sr., and my parents, Troy and Shirley Greene,

Thank you all for giving me the foundation to become the woman that I am today. Each of you taught me something very valuable during my upbringing that was necessary for my journey. I will never despise the fact that I had to experience the back side of the mountain (Marianna, AR) in order to become the woman I am today for such a time as this!

To Mama K (Sandra Spencer),

Thank you for being the mother-in-law you were to me in spite of all that you had to endure with Steve and me during the dark paths our lives took. Whatever path we took, we dragged you right along with us. Thank you for loving and respecting our marriage no matter what. Most importantly, thank you for allowing me to release my heart into this book and for understanding that it is liberation for me! There was never a doubt in my mind that you loved me as your own daughter, and I still believe that till today.

To Granny Rose, my spiritual advisor and prayer warrior,

Thank you for being a woman of faith, and full of WISDOM! I don't know how I would have made it in all of the experiences I endured without your spiritual guidance. You never judged, and you never chose sides in any of our madness. Thank you for loving me right where I was, and coaching me into being the woman of God I am today. You released your mantle and I graciously accept! You will always be my Number One HERO!

To my love Ernest Moorer,

Thank you for understanding this chapter of my life. You have been very supportive from the day the Lord sent you into my life. You have been a breath of fresh air, a glimpse of hope, and a ray of sunshine. Thank you for accepting the good, the bad and the ugly parts of my life and still loving me. I look forward to sharing many more years of happiness with you!

Finally, to those of you who have experienced similar life adversities or are currently in a situation that seems hopeless: This book was written for you to understand that you too can WIN!

Acknowledgements

Truth is liberation to the soul ... and I must admit that writing this book truly marked my freedom from my past. I am grateful to God for giving me the courage to admit my faults openly, without condemnation. I am forever thankful for God's grace, which is sufficient in ALL things.

I thank my Changed Life International Ministries family for praying with me through all the tough times of my life and not judging me along the way. You really gave me hope.

I am truly grateful to the best spiritual father anyone could ever ask for. Thank you, Bishop D. Anthony Robinson, for trusting me to shepherd such a wonderful flock at Changed Life. Even in my brokenness, you saw something great in me.

I also offer my greatest appreciation to my editor, Helaine R. Williams of Make It Plain Ministries. Thank you for countless hours of providing the best service anyone could ask for. Thank you for your creativity, and most importantly, encouraging me throughout this entire project. You are the BEST!

And lastly, I thank the Greene family for being so supportive and loving, no matter what. I give special thanks to my sisters, Stacy, Crystal and Juanita; and to my brothers, Troy and Donny. I love you all more than you know!

*I*Still *Win: a Life of Love, Tragedy, and Triumph* is a labor of love. It takes a strong heart to live and persevere through life's challenges and obstacles. But to revisit each struggle, each lonely night, each day where you simply didn't know if you were going to make it — then to put it all on paper for someone else to learn from it — is exceptional. The transparency alone speaks volumes as to the intent of the book. It has been designed as a tool for others to read and understand that they are not the only ones, nor will they be the last ones, to survive adversity or difficult days.

Pastor Tiffany S. Greene is a 21st-century leader who has been appointed by God for a season such as this. Her strength, courage and integrity are at impeccable. She loves her family, as you will soon find out. She is highly respected in her local church and community. God smiles on her. As you enjoy this book, I encourage you to free your mind to allow yourself to feel the love that fills each page. Know that you, too can win; the place you are in now is temporary, and greater is coming.

— Bishop D. Anthony Robinson

Changed Life International Ministries

North Little Rock, AR

Table of Contents

INTRODUCTION

What do you do when the unthinkable happens? Not just one isolated incident, but a number of unthinkable situations ... especially when they happen all at once? What do you do when satan spends years setting you up for destruction, and then launches simultaneous missile attacks to finish you off in a big fireball? How do you survive this?

Many, like Job in the Old Testament of the Holy Bible, would likely have a close relative at their shoulder, urging them to "curse God and die" as Job's wife suggested he do in Job 2:9. Sure enough, many would lie down and throw in the towel. Some would end up permanently in mental wards. Tragically, some would turn their frustration into a mass murder-suicide. There are so many endless negative possibilities.

Even Christians forget that when Job was tested by satan and in quick succession lost everything — ev-uh-ry-THING, including his health — he did not turn his back on God. Despite all that satan threw at him, including friends who kicked him while he was down, he remained true to the One who had consented to his testing. Indeed, Job 1:22 shows that "In all this, Job sinned not, nor charged God foolishly." In Chapter 2, Verse 10, Job rejected his wife's suggestion, telling her, "Thou speakest as one of the foolish women speaketh. What? Shall we receive good at the hand of God, and shall we not receive evil?" The verse goes on to repeat that "in all this did not Job sin with his lips." As a result, God blessed Job with much more than he had lost, according to Job 42:10-13; 16:

And the LORD turned the captivity of Job, when he prayed for his friends: also the LORD gave Job twice as much as he had before. Then came there unto him all his brethren, and all his sisters, and all they that had been of his acquaintance before, and did eat bread with him in his house: and they bemoaned him, and comforted him over all the evil that the LORD had brought upon him: every man also gave him a piece of money, and everyone an earring of gold. So the LORD blessed the latter end of Job more than his beginning: for he had fourteen thousand sheep, and six thousand camels, and a thousand yoke of oxen, and a thousand she asses. He had also seven sons and three daughters. ... After this lived Job an hundred and forty years, and saw his sons, and his sons' sons, even four generations.

Having gone through some unthinkable things — and being a pastor — I knew I had to write this book. For some time, I had been journaling about my experiences, putting to paper some things the Lord had put in my heart. But I kept sensing that it wasn't time to release these things yet. Let me say here that, sometimes we release things at the wrong time. We release them when we're not completely healed from our spiritual, mental, and emotional traumas. God had to take me through a transition to get me to understand that I had to be patient.

Sometimes, when we're going through what seem to be unbearable situations, we begin to think that God has forgotten us. It's a wrong way to think. God hasn't forgotten us; He's doing a work within us! That work takes time; it's a process. I was really going through a metamorphosis. Although God was allowing me glimpses of aspects of His plan for me, I wasn't ready to come out of the cocoon. See, if a butterfly comes out of its cocoon before its time, it won't develop into a butterfly. It will just be a liquefied mess. God had to show me how messed up it would have been had I come out and shared some things out of time. Season is so important! The Bible tells us, in Ecclesiastes 3:1, that there is a time and season for everything. And I had to realize that what God was showing me wasn't just about me. It wasn't just about my desire to release a book.

When we're going through tribulation, we're often in a dark place and we can't get beyond it. All we can see at that moment is what's right in front of us, not realizing that God has something greater on the other side of our valley. I had to realize there was a process God was taking me through. My struggles with my family — my husband, my children — they all were a part of that process. But I couldn't see beyond my dark place. All I could see was the hurt and pain that I was going through at that particular time.

I know that it's now time for this message to be released. Now that I'm on the other side of my valley, I can look back and say, "Oh! God, THAT'S what you were doing!" Even today, when I'm counseling couples as a pastor, I wonder, "God, how do You still send people my way after all the mistakes and failures of my marriage? Why do You still trust me to minister to someone?" God replied, "Because you can minister to someone in a place you've been." It's hard for you to minister to someone who's in a place you've never been before. I can't minister to you about how to stand in a marriage in which you feel broken, and tell you how God can restore you in that marriage, if I've never been broken! It's tough to minister to someone in that particular place.

I've had experiences that I thought meant the end of the world. I thought the enemy was going to be successful in destroying me. I owe my survival in a large part to the fact that I was finally able to see the big picture. When we go through trials and tribulation, we have to see exactly what God is trying to teach us at that particular moment. I think that oftentimes, the reason we fail to rise above our situations is that we're too busy looking at the tragedy and not at the possibility of a triumph. We're focused on the confusion that's going on, and we can't even begin to see that God wants to turn our mess into an opportunity for Him to bless!

My prayer is that this book will encourage those of you who have lost hope. You can regain your strength and take back the peace and the joy that satan has worked so hard to rob you of. You can be among those the Bible refers to in Isaiah 40:31: "But they that wait upon the LORD shall renew their strength; they shall mount up with wings as eagles; they shall run, and not be weary; and they shall walk, and not faint."

Chapter One

How Did I Get Here?

Sometimes I think back on the times I felt devastated over my circumstances. Life seemed hopeless, and I couldn't understand how God was going to bring me out of my sense of hopelessness. Many people, if they've ever been in such a place, don't know or understand how they got there. What first put me on my slippery slope to hopelessness was the loss of my 2-year-old son, Stephen Robinson Jr., or Li'l Steve, as we often called him. That's when the enemy began to try to destroy me as a person. You see, satan fights ugly. After Li'l Steve's death, the enemy played mind games on me. I was only 21 years old and had no idea I was struggling with demonic spirits amidst my grief.

I first came to Arkansas when my family moved from St. Louis to North Little Rock in 1983. My mother and father were good and loving people, but they were dealing with a lot of issues, including addiction and financial problems. I was aware of that at a really young age; it was an unhealthy environment. This is why at age 13, I moved to Marianna to live with my grandparents. That's when I started the "raised in the church" phase of my life. My grandfather introduced me to the Lord and instilled a sense of values in me. He was the one I looked up to. He was a great example to me, and gave me hope at a time when I didn't feel like I had any sense of a family structure.

It was also around age 13 that I knew something was different about me. I would often visualize myself, speaking up to people in a church setting. I was always amazed by the ability to make an impact on someone else's life. I never had a problem with talking or communicating. I always wanted to be in front of people expressing myself. I didn't know the impact of this vision. I didn't know exactly what God was going to do with it. But the vision was there. I'd had an encounter with God at a young age through this vision.

Sadly, by the time I was 21, I lost that vision. It had been clouded by the things that were happening in my life. Oftentimes, difficult circumstances will leave us standing at a crossroads. We can either decide to allow those circumstances to make us a victim, or we can keep fighting and become the victor. I allowed myself to become a victim, and as a result I put myself on satan's slow boat to destruction.

At the age of 16, I moved back to North Little Rock with my parents, brothers and sisters. Because I'd had a different upbringing those three years in Marianna, I didn't feel a connection with my immediate family. As a matter of fact, I felt like an outcast.

I enrolled in Sylvan Hills High School, where I met my husband, Stephen "Steve" Robinson, and we began dating. My life seemed to move so fast at this time because I was now doing things that would not have been allowed at my grandparents' house. I had more freedom, and I did not channel this freedom in the right direction. As a result, I became pregnant with Steve's child at 18, and we were married. After we graduated from Sylvan Hills, Steve enlisted in the Army. I followed him, and we began our lives as young adults with a new baby.

Li'l Steve was born June 18, 1991. He was a very vibrant, loving little boy. We were very proud of our son. He was very inquisitive and certainly impressionable when it came to his father. Today, when I think of the conversations we had with him, I see it was apparent that he would grow up to be a very intelligent man.

After Steve served two years at Fort Riley, Kansas our duty station was changed to Ft. Benning, Ga. By this time, I was pregnant with our second child. Life was certainly moving faster than I had anticipated. When I look back at this time in my life, I must admit that I was scared. We were young, inexperienced, and away from home. Neither of us had any idea how to be married or raise children. We were just two kids in love with each other, trying to make the best of life.

On Feb. 10, 1994, I gave birth to my second son, Dion. I can remember Li'l Steve being so happy to have a little brother! He was fascinated with Dion's little hands and feet. He would ask to hold the baby and was very helpful when it came to getting Dion's bottle and diapers ready. "I'm a big boy, Mama!" he'd say. I still remember those moments just like yesterday.

Now having none of my family around to help me with both children, I was exhausted. Not only was I totally exhausted, I felt lonely. I felt I had a lot of responsibility on me at such a young age, but I didn't really know how to be a mother. I had not been taught how to mother; I had little or no experience. However, I was happy to have my sons. I didn't know all the right things to do, but I was determined to raise them the best way I knew.

It was nine days after I gave birth to Dion that tragedy struck our family.

The day of the accident — Feb. 19, 1994 — my husband suggested he take Li'l Steve out for a ballgame at the park. I was pleased as well as relieved to get a break from taking care of both a newborn and a toddler. Li'l Steve was also excited.

They left, leaving me with Dion. The day went on. Steve and Li'l Steve did not come home after the game. There was no phone call from Steve. I became worried. I tried to call him — no answer. At this point I started wondering, *What's going on?*

About 6 o'clock that evening, I got a knock on my door. It was my husband's commanding officer. He told me Steve had been in a car accident. I was frantic.

The officer told me to gather up some things to come to the hospital, which I did. My baby and I got in the commanding officer's car. On the way to the hospital, I prayed intensely for my husband and child. I didn't know the extent of the accident, but I knew something was not right.

When I got to the hospital, the nurse and doctors came in and began telling me all the things that were wrong with my husband ... the lacerations in his leg and his other injuries. I was relieved that he was alive, but my thoughts were on Li'l Steve.

"OK, what about my son? Where is my son?" I asked them.

"Ma'am, just calm down," the doctor said. "We're going to go into this with you."

"No, I need to know what is going on with my child," I insisted.

"Ma'am, I'm sorry; your son didn't make it," the doctor said.

He went on to tell me that Steve had hit a tree. My son had been ejected from the truck and had died on impact.

Oh my God, how did this happen? I wondered.

There was no explanation as to how it happened. To this day, all I know is that my husband lost control of the truck and that my son was not in a car seat. A friend of my husband had gone along. The truck Steve was driving was a small Chevrolet S10 pickup truck. There was not enough room in the cab for both the car seat and an adult passenger. So Steve and his friend took Li'l Steve out of the car seat and put him between them. Actually, when Steve hit the tree, all three of them had been ejected from the truck. But Li'l Steve was thrown against the tree.

There were so many emotions I was experiencing a 21-year-old wife and mother. But one emotion in particular began to stand out: anger I began to feel anger like I've never felt it before. I was angry with life. Angry with my husband, angry with God because I knew Him ... because I'd had a relationship with Him ... yet, He'd allowed this to happen to me.

This is where I found myself at the crossroads, with the one path leading to hopelessness. I took that path. For a long time, I shut myself off to the notion of a relationship with God. It was the first time in my life that I felt so much grief and despair.

One might say, "Well, your husband is alive. You have a 2-week-old child. You can bounce back from this." And after some time had passed, many people did say something to that effect. They wanted to know why I was still in grief.

My problem was that I didn't understand how to process grief; how to let go. I think this is what a lot of people deal with, whether it be death, betrayal, or someone else's mistreatment of them. When you don't know how to process grief, you do all the wrong things.

Heavenly Father, we know that You do not put tragedy on us. We don't fully understand why certain things are allowed to happen, but we know You are there to comfort those of us who mourn, and get us through the valley. We ask that you enfold us with Your loving arms during tough and tragic times; dry our tears, help us to grieve healthfully and — as you have done in infinite cases — bring out whatever good can result from bad things. In Jesus' name, Amen.

Chapter Two

Trapped in the Blaming Game

Grief takes you through several things, all of which I felt. After Li'l Steve's death, I felt guilty. In a situation such as this, you begin wondering what you might have done forehand to prevent tragedy, and sure enough, I began to self-interrogate and self-accuse: *Did I do the right thing that day? Should I have allowed Li'l Steve to go to the game? What could I have done differently? Maybe if I hadn't felt so tired, Steve wouldn't have felt so responsible for taking him.*

After you go through all of this guilt process, you begin the blame game. So I began to blame my husband. I thought, *Well, if you had just had the seat belt on, this wouldn't have happened.* Now who's to say that it wouldn't have happened anyway? None of us can really predict how and why situations are, or the direction in which they'll go. But remember, I was young. Even some older people fail to process their grief correctly. When you don't process grief right, you find yourself in a whole different situation ... and I did not process my grief right for many years. So I was angry with Steve, still angry with myself, and angry with anyone else as well as anything that reminded me of the day of the accident. And, again, I was angry with God. I couldn't understand why He would allow my son to be taken from me. I felt this righteous indignation.

Eventually my anger turned into bitterness. I became furious with my family when they began to move on, although they knew I was still hurt. My attitude was, *How could everybody move on despite all that happened? How could everybody be OK?* I began to wonder the same thing about my husband: *How could he move on? How could all of this be OK with him?*

What I didn't realize was that he was masking his own pain from the loss. He was masking it through infidelity.

The enemy had begun to divide and conquer us. Division and separation are one of his most powerful weapons. Ever since satan himself rebelled against God and split the angels in heaven (Jude 1:6; Rev. 12:4, 12:9), he has worked to destroy or dilute anything Godly through division, from churches to marriages.

The Bible has a definite word about the value of unity, and the dire consequences of division. Psalm 133:1 starts out, " ... Behold, how good and how pleasant *it is* for brethren to dwell together in unity!" Unity is held in such value by the psalm writer that in Verse 2-3, he compares it to "the precious ointment upon the head, that ran down upon the beard, even Aaron's beard: that went down to the skirts of his garments; As the dew of Hermon, and as the dew that descended upon the mountains of Zion: for there the LORD commanded the blessing, even life for evermore." Amos 3:3 asks, "Can two walk together, except they be agreed?" And in Mark 3: 24-25, Jesus addressed the scribes who were suspicious of Him casting out demons in the name of Beelzebub: " ... If a kingdom be divided against itself, that kingdom cannot stand. And if a house be divided against itself, that house cannot stand."

A marriage is a union of two people. If there is no unity within the union, there cannot be a successful marriage.

So, I wasn't dealing with my grief properly, Steve wasn't dealing with his grief properly, and we were not being honest with each other. Out of this dynamic came hopelessness. I felt our relationship, our marriage, was hopeless. Not only that, I felt life itself was hopeless.

Over a period of time, my feelings of guilt, anger and bitterness were eventually joined by feelings of shame. The enemy was telling me, "If you'd have been a better mother, you wouldn't be going through this," so anytime anybody asked me what happened, I was *embarrassed* to talk about it. It's sad, because talking is what I really needed to do!

But instead of talking about it, I held it in. Now, this is what satan likes to do. He likes to get us to cover up pain, to mask it. That's how he can begin to build strongholds in our minds, one on top of the other on top of the other ... not just poisoning our minds, but essentially building a fortress that hardens the heart. He began to build bricks around my heart as well as Steve's heart. Any time I looked at him, I saw my pain instead of seeing the love I had for him. I saw misery. And I began to harbor unforgiveness.

The enemy had played the accident in my mind as though I was there. This was a *mind battle*. That's why I say, as the Bible says in 2 Cor. 10:5, that we must stay about the business of "casting down imaginations, and every high thing that exalteth itself against the knowledge of God, and bringing into captivity every thought to the obedience of Christ." I wasn't doing that.

I became obsessed with my son's death, I found out exactly where the accident happened so that I could go back to the site. I drove there, looked at the area, and looked at the tree. I thought I was finding solace and healing and closure. But the enemy was setting me up to see an "imagination" — a tape that for many years I replayed in my mind, as though I had witnessed the accident. It was just a way satan was trying to keep me in bondage, to keep me angry, to harden my heart. A tragedy that should have brought my husband and me closer together, instead drove a wedge between us. That wedge began to take over our marriage as time passed.

When the grief of losing a child is not handled properly, it can cause so many other issues — not just in your marriage, but in other areas of your everyday life. There's no way you can be prosperous. There's no way you can see your purpose in life. You can't even begin to see victory in a particular situation as long as you mask your pain. Once I was delivered, God showed me so many things I was supposed to have done at that time that would have led to my being healed sooner. But I missed these opportunities.

Let me inject here one thing people shouldn't say to mothers who have lost a child. Definitely don't tell them, "You have other children," as though the surviving children would take the place of the deceased child! Also, understand that the timing of everyone's grieving process is not the same. I had to say this so many times to my family members because they could not comprehend why I was still grieving. Many of them would tell me, "You've got the other child to take care of."

Angela Morrow, a registered nurse and expert on dying, funerals and grief, discusses the grieving process in an About.com article, "Grief and Mourning: What's Normal and What's Not?: Normal Grief and Complicated Grief." She writes that "grief is a bereaved person's internal emotional response to the loss event. It has several components: physical, behavioural, emotional, mental, social, and spiritual. It is often described by those that have gone through it as a heaviness that isn't easily lifted. It can sometimes be so pronounced that it affects a person's physical self and can even mimic illnesses." Morrow's article contains a link to a related About. com article, "When Grief Gets Complicated." Here, mental health expert Leonard Holmes writes about complicated grief, a severe grief that can "reach the level of a mental disorder." Holmes cites a July 2005 study published in the *Journal of the American Medical Association* concerning the treatment of complicated grief, described as:

"A sense of disbelief regarding the death;

Anger and bitterness over the death;

Recurrent pangs of painful emotions, with intense yearning and longing for the deceased;

Preoccupation with thoughts of the loved one, often including distressing intrusive thoughts related to the death. (Shear, et. al., 2005)"

Even in the case of "healthy" grief, everybody's grieving process is not the same. And my grief was complicated. Yes, I allowed my feelings to fester and become spiritual strongholds. But it would also have been a mistake for me to refuse to acknowledge and work through the anger, the guilt, the helplessness, the bitterness and the shame; freedom would not have come. God gave us emotions and they are very important for the body — as a matter of fact, they're a part of our souls. We have to be able to release and express our emotions. If we don't, we'll "stroke out." We will react in ways that aren't good for our bodies.

And although depression is not good for the body, depression is so very real. I think many in the Body of Christ just don't want to deal with the fact that so many saints have dealt with depression. So many people end up abusing their bodies, or otherwise expressing themselves inappropriately, even killing themselves, because they refuse to deal with their emotions by going through the grieving process. I think our emotional processes are necessary for us to have an effective life. Everything has to be done in balance, and in its own time. But the people around me wanted to hurry me up: "You're still grieving? How long will you continue to go through that process?" Sometimes people think they're being supportive of you, but they're not. So I found myself seeking the wrong kind of support.

Precious Lord, we know your Word says to be angry but sin not. We ask that you help us keep our anger in check and, especially, refrain from allowing satan to use misguided anger to eat us up and poison spiritually, mentally, emotionally, relationally and physically. We ask for victory over the mind battles the enemy may declare on us; the manifestation of healing from any pain we may be suffering; and the strength not to let our pain fester into anger and our anger fester into disunity in our marriages or other relationships. We ask this in Jesus' name. Amen.

Chapter Three

Processing the Pain

Steve was honorably discharged from the Army in August 1994 and we returned to Arkansas to live. We settled in, but we were not settled.

We both masked our pain. Steve saw other women; I became a closet drinker. Whenever I got off from work or anytime I was alone, I drank. I would go to the liquor store and get a fifth of Crown Royal to have some tucked away at home so nobody would know what I was doing. When Steve left the house, I was actually relieved, because that was my drinking time. I would go in our bedroom and drink my sorrows away. Mind you, I had a child at the time. I believe Dion knew about my drinking. He never said anything to me, but I believe he knew. He was a young child who wanted his mother's attention. Imagine him, tucked away in his room watching TV and playing games while Mom's in her room getting drunk and Dad is in the streets doing his own thing.

For a while I'd call Steve to find out where he was and try to get him to come home. It's sad to say, but I got to a point where it didn't matter to me whether he came home or not. I wanted to be left alone anyway.

I don't think my parents and other family members had a clue as to my drinking. My dad was an alcoholic and drug addict when I grew up, so I knew alcoholism ran in my family and I knew it was a trap that would be all too easy for me to fall into. But at this time I saw it as my source of healing. I felt I could drink my sorrows away — or so I thought. That's a myth, too, because the more drunker you get, the more you think about your problems ... and the more they hurt. The more pain you feel, the more you drink. So alcohol just starts a vicious cycle. It doesn't "drown out" anything! But the enemy makes you think that if you get just a little bit more drunk, you'll be fine.

With all this going on, my marriage was on life support. The trust was gone. We communicated by arguing. But we remained together. I believe Steve stayed only because he felt a sense of responsibility, as well as guilt over Li'l Steve's death. I didn't want to leave, because Steve's infidelity left me with a sense of rejection. I already felt hopeless. The pain from the loss of my child was so overwhelming; I didn't have the strength to do anything different.

What I had the strength to do was pretend everything was OK. By doing that, I didn't realize at the time exactly how much I was hurting Steve AND me. We were both hurting each other, actually. We were practically growing up together, in our early 20s, going through the motions of being a family. I was self-destructing, Steve was self-destructing. And Dion was in the middle of the chaos. It got to the point to where he would ask questions, because you can hide things from a child for only so long before he figures that something is not right.

Ironically, we were in church this entire time. When we returned to Arkansas we began going to Steve's home church, but we were not very active there. Unfortunately, the leadership and the spiritual guidance we both needed were not there. No one sat us down and said, "You guys need some help. You both are not only self-destructing; you've got your child in the middle of this self-destruction."

Despite our problems, I had this longing to have another baby. But my body would not cooperate. I had a disease called endometriosis. I became pregnant several times, but miscarried. I believe I wanted to have this baby because, having still not healed from Li'l Steve's death, I felt I needed something to hold on to.

As it was, I was holding on to Dion, but not in a healthy manner. He was older by this time — 4 or 5 — and the enemy had begun to play with my mind, convincing me that something was going to happen to him. I was still dealing with the loss of one child and feared losing another, so I became overprotective. I couldn't bear not knowing where he was, so I didn't want him to go anywhere, let alone spend the night at anybody else's house. I would wake up in the middle of the night, sometimes in a cold sweat, worried about Dion. I'd get up and run to his room to check on him. There I was, pouring all this negative energy into my child as I continued to grieve for his brother and continued to try, unsuccessfully, to have another baby.

A new child did come into my life, but not the way I'd hoped. One day, I got an anonymous call at work. The caller told me that Steve had gotten another woman pregnant.

When I asked him about it, he denied it. But when we went to the hospital he saw that the baby, Terrance, looked like him. Steve then admitted that Terrance was his son. For me, that was pain on top of pain: The pain of losing a child four years earlier, and my failure to heal; the pain of my inability to carry a baby to term. And now, the pain of knowing that another woman became pregnant with my husband's seed and gave birth to his son. Once again I felt this sense of shame. *How do I deal with remaining married to someone who not only has been unfaithful to me, but now has another woman's child to show for it? I wondered.*

Steve and I talked. He told me that if we were going to make our marriage work, I would have to accept Terrance. His viewpoint was this: "The mistake was made. I did it, I apologize and this is where we are.

Now we need to know whether you will be able to stay with me." I understood that, but my pain was great from all that had happened.

We began to go for counseling ... not so much for us to deal with Steve's infidelity, but for me to deal with whether or not I'd be able to remain in the marriage. The good thing was that my healing process did get its start. We received some really good counseling from a couple in Little Rock. We began to find out that Steve's infidelity was his way of masking his pain. And the way I was masking my pain was not just by drinking. I'd also been pushing Steve away from me, not wanting him to touch me, not wanting him to be around me. I hated the thought of him being in the same room with me. I had been in a really, really, *really* dark place.

I realized that we were two young adults who were really messed up and needed help. And I knew I just couldn't use this particular situation to end the marriage. I realized yes, this was a bad situation; it was bad that we had to come to this point to get the help we needed. But divorce was not an option for me.

Not everybody can come to this conclusion. Some people decide, "I can't remain in a marriage to someone who has been unfaithful to me." You have to decide for yourself how much you are able to handle. You have to know where you stand; mentally and emotionally.

I don't condone infidelity in any marriage. But I understand the extent to which we can act out on the basis of the pain that we're trying to mask. Steve acted out, and his actions brought about a child. I acted out by doing such things as drinking and driving, which could have resulted in my death and/or someone else's.

It doesn't matter how it happens, pain is pain. I don't condone Steve's actions or mine ... which is why over time, I could forgive. That was the start of my healing process. This process took time; it took me dealing with me. I actually had to stop looking at the circumstances and focus only on God and His restoration work on me. This is when my turning point began.

Father of Glory, father of lights, we all have a God-shaped hole in us that only You can fill. We ask that You help us yield not to the temptation to try to fill that hole with substitutes that are not only woefully inadequate, but that will ultimately destroy us, let alone adversely affect our children, which You have entrusted to our care. As speaking spirits with authority, we hereby bind the spirit of addiction, loose its would-be satanic results, and release the fullness of the Spirit of love and Spirit of Truth into our lives. Lord, we thank You for completeness in You. In Jesus' precious name, Amen.

Chapter Four

In-To-Me-See
(True Intimacy with God)

It's funny that it took something like Steve fathering a child with another woman for my healing to begin. But this is when I began to really want to seek within me to find out where this pain was coming from and how I could get past *me* in order to begin to work on my marriage. There was no way I could work on my marriage in the state that I was in ... without dealing with me.

My healing process was definitely a "come to Jesus meeting" for me. I had to really search within myself and say, "God, this is something that is far more out of my control than I could even imagine." Here I am, dealing with pain as a woman who has lost a child, could not have another child, and will have to accept a child my husband fathered. All of that, at the time, seemed to be so much to bear. We don't understand sometimes why things happen the way they do and why God allows us to go through certain processes. Looking back, I now understand why I had to "go through." He had a work that He was doing in me.

As part of this process, I began to look at the word *intimacy*. Break down the word, and you have "in-to-me-see." It is so profound to me. This time was when I actually began to see into me. I didn't have any intimacy with *me;* in other words, I didn't love *me.* I didn't love who I was. I had lost me back in February 1994, and had stayed lost. I had relived that particular situation so much that I lost me. I couldn't even begin to see the desires that I had for me. I had no respect for myself anymore. I had no sense of self-worth. My self-esteem was at the lowest point. I had PTSD — post-traumatic stress disorder, described on the Web as "a condition of persistent mental and emotional stress occurring as a result of injury or severe psychological shock, typically involving disturbance of sleep and constant vivid recall of the experience, with dulled responses to others and to the outside world."

In addition, I wasn't mothering my child, Dion, as I was supposed to mother him. I had pretty much become a lord over him instead of loving him and nurturing him as a mother is supposed to nurture a child. I saw myself as the person who was hired to protect his every move instead of someone who was nurturing his journey. There's a difference between nurturing a person's journey and micromanaging his every step. I had my finger and my thumb on every move of his, simply because there was a problem within *me.* I had allowed Li'l Steve's death to overwhelm me so much that I lost me, and as a result I had no real relationship with Dion. I lost the chance to properly nurture him for the first five or six years of his life.

God showed me all this. He then said, "You don't even know who I am. You don't have any idea of who I really am. You lost that idea a long time ago."

I'd allowed myself to become a victim. And I turned against my own husband — treating him as if he'd *wanted* something tragic to happen to his own child.

We do this so often in our relationships. We become victims of situations in our lives and expect those around us to play along when we put on our victim masks. That's what I basically did to my family. I wanted them to see me as a victim. I wanted my family to see me as the one who was hurt, and everybody else needed to know I was hurt.

The enemy had piled one weapon on top of another. As I look back with opened eyes, I can just see them piling up ... hopelessness, then fear, then low self-esteem, then a sense of worthlessness. I didn't realize how many weapons I was buried in, until I began to accept God's offer of intimacy. And as I became intimate with Him, I began to see *me*. I looked in the mirror and I saw how ugly I was. I could actually see those spirits ... hopelessness, distress, low self-esteem. I began to wonder, "How did this happen?" I had once been vibrant, happy and outgoing, able to talk to people easily. Now I was this secluded, depressed woman whose self-esteem was nearly non-existent.

God took me on a journey to see within me so that I would realize just how messed up I really was. This is when the transition happened for me. This is when I stopped blaming Steve. All these years, I'd had no idea how much he was going through internally. I had been regarding him as the enemy when we should have come together and I should have seen the *enemy* as the enemy! It's so awful how satan tries to destroy families that way.

At this point, I began to go into what I'll call "extreme closet-prayer sessions." I was walking around in my house, praying. A shift had taken place. When the shift happened, I didn't have the desire to spend time dwelling on where Steve might be and what he might be doing. My desire shifted to searching God's Word. His Word became so alive in my spirit. It became water to my soul, and I was thirsty. It was a transition, kind of like Saul's conversion to the Apostle Paul after his experience on the road to Damascus in Acts 9. The scales were pulled from my eyes, and I could really see. "Oh my God, satan has had me blind — and I don't know how to find my way!" I cried out. I prayed for deliverance from all the anger, bitterness, resentfulness and unforgiveness I had toward my husband.

God took me all the way back to where my pain originally began. I think that's what happens with us; we don't go all the way back to the root of our problem. If we're going to get healing, we have to pull up the root. If we don't, that problem is going to spring up again. When it springs up again, it's going to come back seven times worse than what it was before. I had to go back to the root of the cause ... to the point that I even lost focus on the issue of the son Steve had fathered outside our marriage. People's opinions didn't matter to me. What mattered to me at this point was me being healed. So, six years after the accident, I checked myself into a private mental hospital.

Let me make this point: We, as the body of Christ, have a real problem with our willingness to deal with our issues through counseling! People are so private — "I don't want anybody in my business," "I keep folks out of my business." If I had not gone to that place and gotten the help I needed from skilled people, I hate to think of where I might have ended up. I believe God gives us knowledge, gifts and talents to enable us to do what we do on earth. I was given the opportunity to get before some skilled people who could stabilize me, get me the healing I needed.

Now checking into a mental hospital is something a lot of people don't like to talk about. It was a very trying time; it was also a very embarrassing time. The enemy tried to make me ashamed, and for a long time I didn't let anybody know where I'd gone.

People just thought I went on a vacation or went on hiatus.

But it was necessary for me to go into that healing place. My mind had been cluttered with so many different things — trying to process my grief, not understanding how to process my grief. When people experience traumatic events for the first time in their lives, and don't know how to process their grief, they sometimes react in all the wrong ways and find themselves in some dark places. When I checked myself into the hospital, I was able to understand that I wasn't the only one going through this type of ordeal. I met with others who were experiencing "complicated" grief after losing loved ones.

Alone in my hospital room, I found myself being broken down to where God could really deal with me. One night I was on the floor, asking Him, "Why did I end up in this place? What is Your purpose for my pain? Why am I going through this? Why can't I see myself through this process?" I'd known God. I'd begun my relationship with Him at a young age. But I hadn't talked to Him in a long time. It's a very difficult place to be in when you realize that although you *know* God, you *know* you are saved — you'd never had a true, intimate relationship with Him. As He'd told me, I didn't know who He was! This is where I found myself ... looking for intimacy with Him, trying to find answers, trying to figure out how to connect to what God was trying to show me.

I began to cry out to Him. I explained to Him how I was feeling. I told Him how angry I was. How angry I was at Him. How angry I was to have to experience something like this at such a young age, not knowing what to do and being unable to even understand *how* to hear His voice.

God answered by taking me through some Scriptures. One Scripture in particular was Matthew 5:4: "Blessed are those who mourn, for they will be comforted." This Scripture helped me understand that it's OK to grieve, whether those around you have compassion for you during the process or not. (Some people will last with you after the funeral and maybe even a few months later, but eventually they'll get back to their lives and you're left alone trying to pick up the pieces.)

Who will comfort those who mourn? I was also led to 2 Corinthians 1:3-4: "Blessed be God, even the Father of our Lord Jesus Christ, the Father of mercies, and the God of all comfort; Who comforteth us in all our tribulation, that we may be able to comfort them which are in any trouble, by the comfort wherewith we ourselves are comforted of God." This Scripture helped me to understand that God is the Father of compassion and the God of ALL comfort! He knew exactly where I was and could reach me in this low place where people couldn't. This Scripture gave me hope that His compassion would go beyond what others could give me.

Then there was 1 Thessalonians 4:13-18, which gave me hope that as a believer, I would one day see my son Li'l Steve again! I still lean on this Scripture today whenever I get down about the loss of my son and other family members.

> But I would not have you to be ignorant, brethren, concerning them which are asleep, that ye sorrow not, even as others which have no hope. For if we believe that Jesus died and rose again, even so, them also which sleep in Jesus will God bring with him. For this we say unto you by the Word of the Lord, that we which are alive and remain unto the coming of the Lord shall not prevent them which are asleep. For the Lord himself shall descend from heaven with a shout, with the voice of the archangel, and with the trump of God: and the dead in Christ shall rise first: Then we which are alive and remain shall be caught up together with them in the clouds, to meet the Lord in the air: and so shall we ever be with the Lord. Wherefore comfort one another with these words.

Sometimes as believers, we begin to feel as if even God has forgotten us in our dark places. There was a time I felt lost and alone, and at some points, angry at God. I was in the hospital dealing with depression and God led me to these Scriptures. They spoke such volumes to me that I fell on my knees and asked God to forgive me for assuming that He had left me, and accusing Him of bringing life-destroying grief upon me. I must say that God did allow these things to happen in my life, but I had to get to the place of understanding that it was not His will to bring affliction or grief to me. He did not leave me ... He was always there.

Another Scripture that brought comfort was Lamentations 3:31-33: "For the Lord will not cast off for ever: But though he cause grief, yet will he have compassion according to the multitude of his mercies. For he doth not afflict willingly nor grieve the children of men." Even if the Lord's chastening is the source of our grief, it won't last forever. His love for us will prompt Him to show His compassion for us and dry our tears.

Yet another Scripture was Psalm 34:18: "The LORD is nigh unto them that are of a broken heart; and saveth such as be of a contrite spirit." With this Scripture brought further realization that God would save me from the feeling of hopelessness. He was still close to me, even though I felt my spirit was so crushed that I didn't matter anymore.

The healing I received from God wasn't mental healing, it was spiritual healing. I began to understand that it wasn't His desire for me to continue to harbor my anguish. The grief is part of the process. The range of emotions is part of the process. But it wasn't God's desire for me to be stuck in this place.

I was being introduced to my spirit man, that incorruptible "saved" part of us that emerges after we accept Christ and our "old man," or old sin nature, dies, as the Apostle Paul explains in Romans 6. I was being shown how to be *led* by my spirit man, rather than be stuck in the soulish realm (my emotions).

Sometimes people don't understand the difference between our spirit man and our soulish realm. On the website Gotquestions.org, in answer to the question "What is the difference between the soul and spirit of man?," the author of the answer points out that:

> The word "spirit" refers only to the immaterial facet of humanity .... In Paul's writing, the spiritual was pivotal to the life of the believer (1 Corinthians 2:14, 3:1; Ephesians 1:3; 5:19; Colossians 1:9; 3:16). The spirit is the element in humanity which gives us the ability to have an intimate relationship with God. Whenever the word "spirit" is used, it refers to the immaterial part of humanity that "connects" with God, who Himself is spirit (John 4:24). ... The soul is the essence of humanity's being .... The spirit is the aspect of humanity that connects with God.

When I got out of the hospital, I knew I needed to connect to a spiritual source so that I could continue my healing. I was weak, and I *knew* I was weak. Here was another crossroads decision many of us have to make: whether to seek a spiritual encounter, or lose one's self in alcohol, drugs, promiscuity. We're going to make some attempt to fill that hole inside of us, one way or another.

I knew I'd had an encounter with God when I was 13. But I didn't realize that the spiritual *foundation* I received while living with my grandfather would play a major part in my life later on. Because that foundation was there, I could go back to it.

When I went into the private mental institution, they asked this series of questions — "Are you suicidal?," etc. — and they keep you for seven days to make sure you don't do anything to yourself. I knew I was suicidal. I knew that if I didn't get some help I might take my own life. The grief had consumed me that much.

But the joy of all of this is when you can acknowledge that you're in this place. I think what happens is that some people just don't want to admit that they need help. Some people just don't *know* how they feel. Some people just decide that it's better going out than staying in. But I thank God that I knew I needed help and that I knew that I couldn't do it on my own. I knew there was nobody around me who could help, not even in my own family. Even those who'd call and say, "I just wanted to see how you were doing" — none of them could help me. Not even my husband, the one that was supposed to be closest to me. I actually had to pull myself away from that circle of people to seek help. I think that's why it was easier for me, when I did leave the hospital, to receive the spiritual healing that I did.

O Holy One, if we should stray away from You, we ask that you give us no peace until we become intimate with ourselves — in-to-me-see — and become like the Prodigal Son, saying "I will arise and go to my father."

Otherwise, Lord, help us to remember to examine and judge ourselves daily according to Your Word, 1 Cor. 11:31 — "For if we would judge ourselves, we should not be judged." We ask that any healing from current strongholds stemming from dysfunctional family-of-origin dynamics or past traumatic events be made manifest by Jesus' stripes, and that we immerse ourselves in the salve of time spent in your face and in Your Word. Thank you for comforting us when we hurt, and mending our broken hearts. In the name of Jesus the Christ, King of King and Lord of Lords, Amen.

Chapter Five

Healing through the Word

O nce I was released from the hospital, I connected with a wonderful woman of God, Alma Rose Reddick — better known as "Granny Rose' — who served as my spiritual mentor. God used her to begin a spiritual awakening in me, one that I had never experienced before. I began to "eat" the Scriptures, live the Scriptures, and apply the Scriptures to my everyday life.

I became so immersed in the Word that I placed post-it notes with verses on my bathroom mirror. When I got up in the morning and brushed my teeth, I would read a verse of Scripture. I'd particularly focus on 2 Tim. 1:7: "For God hath not given us the spirit of fear; but of power, and of love, and of a sound mind." Regardless of what the enemy is trying to throw at me I know I have a sound mind! I wasn't crazy, I *knew* I wasn't crazy. I was going through a process of grief. In that process, I had to understand there also was a spiritual encounter that God wanted to have with me ... and that the only way I could actually grab on to what God was saying would be through His Word. You cannot hear the voice of God without having His Word; you simply cannot. His Word is His voice. Until I was able to get His Word on the inside of me, all I ever seemed to be able to do was replay, in my mind, Li'l Steve's leaving the house with his daddy the day of the accident and telling me, "I love you Mommy; bye Mommy." That replay tormented me for many years until I decided I was tired of being tormented. We have to understand we're in a spiritual battle. It was a mind game satan was playing against me, but like many people, I didn't realize it at the time; it was difficult to.

The Apostle Paul clearly explains how to combat the enemy's mind games in 2 Cor. 10:4-5.

> **(For the weapons of our warfare are not carnal, but mighty through God to the pulling down of strong holds;) Casting down imaginations, and every high thing that exalteth itself against the knowledge of God, and bringing into captivity every thought to the obedience of Christ.**

Instead of "casting down imaginations, and every high thing that exalteth itself against the knowledge of God, and bringing into captivity every thought to the obedience of Christ," I'd been exalting those imaginations, bringing them further and further into my mindset, and letting them become strongholds. But when I began to get the Word inside of me, then I had the ammunition to win the battle for my mind. And that's what Granny Rose helped me do. She gave me the weapons of warfare, and those weapons saved my life.

Again, I came to realize that God was a God of comfort; that "blessed are they that mourn" that there was nothing wrong with me for mourning; that I was supposed to go through that process. But I also needed to understand the other part of that Scripture — "for they will be comforted." As I started realizing these things, I also began to realize that yes; I *could* connect where I was to where God was trying to take me! I also realized I didn't have to stay in that place of mourning, or of feeling helpless. So a major transition began in my life. I was being restored again! I started to experience a sense of peace due to the application of those Scriptures.

Granny Rose was the one who pointed out to me what had been going on in our marriage. "You are dealing with your pain in one way, and he's dealing with his pain in another," she said.

I realize now that hurting people hurt people. Because I was hurting, I hurt my husband. I lashed out — a lot. I said ugly things to him. I told him that Li'l Steve would still be alive if he hadn't had him out of the car seat. I was tearing him down. I tore him down a lot. And when he pretended to be OK, I was hurt the more because he seemed OK! I felt like we were not on the same page, that he was leaving me alone to grieve by myself. But he wasn't OK. He was still dealing with his pain and his demons.

I made things worse because I was *trying* to hurt him. I wanted him to hurt just as much as I was hurting. It's a sad place we're in when we're hurting the person that's closest to us.

One day, after I decided I wanted to stay and make our marriage work, I asked him, "Why do YOU want to make this marriage work?" (I think this is important for people who are going through marital issues. Each partner needs to understand why the other wants to make the marriage work. Wanting to make the marriage work *only* because that's what the other partner wants, is not the key to restoring the marriage.)

It was when I asked the question that I finally began to see the brokenness in him. He let me know that he never wanted the marriage to end. He said he loved me and wanted to rebuild on our marriage. But he was in pain. He was dealing with some issues and he'd made some mistakes. He knew he would have to rebuild my trust in him and that we were going to have to be honest with one another.

We definitely knew that communication as well as trust, was an issue for us; because we didn't communicate. We knew that if we wanted to make the marriage work, we definitely would have to work hard on this marriage together and now, with a child outside our marriage.

Rebuilding the marriage relationship was the most difficult process of all. Yes, I'd accepted Terrance; yes, Steve and I were going to work on having a blended family. However, it soon became evident that a spirit had attached itself to my husband, causing him to continue his adulterous activities, and it wasn't going to let him go that easily. It's definitely tough when you're trying hard to make your marriage work, but the other party is not delivered from demonic attachments.

Because of these issues, I became consumed with why Steve continued to be in bondage. So again I found myself searching the Word — this time for Scriptures about marital love, especially submitting to one's husband and being there for him.

I couldn't understand why he continued his infidelity. It wasn't even about the loss of my son anymore. It was about me having hope in my marriage, and hope in God, and hope in the Word of God, knowing He could restore. If God could restore me spiritually, mentally and emotionally, surely He could restore our marriage. I was holding on to just that hope. I kept thinking, "God, I cannot be the only believer who is experiencing this."

I'd gotten to the point where I was just dumbfounded. I was lost. I'd hit a brick wall. The good thing was that I'd grown to trust God, staying regular in His presence and in His Word. I asked God to show me the answer to this dilemma. I couldn't see God not showing me an answer to what was going on ... I wanted that answer, whether I stayed in the marriage or whether I got out of the marriage. So I began to research this spirit of promiscuity, of whoredom. I went back to when the adultery began. And I went into prayer and I began to ask God to show me how to handle this particular situation.

I remember discussing this with Steve during one of our sessions with Granny Rose. During this discussion, Steve just began to cry. I saw a side of him that I had not seen before. I saw that he was searching to fill that hole within him but was going about it all the wrong way. He felt he could not trust me because I had hurt him, and he didn't know whether I'd hurt him again.

He revealed that I beat him down mentally to the point that he felt small. When he was around me, he had to pretend to be the Mufasa, the king that he really wanted to be, but he never saw himself as that with me. He explained to me that whenever he was with another woman, *that* woman made him feel like he was like a king. But I would always browbeat him and make him feel insignificant. He saw the pain I was carrying, he said, and he knew he couldn't make me feel like I needed to feel because I had been hurt so bad.

That's when I began to realize that the enemy had used my son's death years earlier to start a major campaign to destroy my life. I had been delivered from the strongholds satan had built in my mind after Li'l Steve's death, but Steve wasn't healed yet, therefore the accident was still causing problems in the marriage. Steve began to let me know that every time he looked at me, he saw my grief, my pain, my emptiness. He always felt that because of this, he could never make me happy. When I was unable to carry another child to term, it bothered him. He wanted us to have another child.

I had no idea of any of this, because we had not been communicating. If you and your spouse do not communicate your feelings to each other, you're headed for marital destitution. You're going to die in that situation. You will have left a place for the enemy to come in, and if you don't communicate, he'll communicate for you! He'll make sure somebody is saying something to you or that one of his demons is whispering something in your ear. Or he'll send somebody to whisper in your spouse's ear. In general, if you fail to deal with the issues that are going on in your marriage — I don't care how minute they may seem — the consequences can be serious.

So, 10 years into our marriage, Steve and I began to pull off some of the layers in which we'd been wrapped. This time of pulling off layers is when I believe the transition happened for him. This is when he began to really seek God for the healing that he needed to receive. I had not seen that happen before. He'd even borne the pain of the loss of our child far longer than I did. I think it hit me harder in some ways, but he held it longer and had been spiralling faster. Not only had he turned to other women, he also turned to alcohol *and* drugs. All this added to the problems that we were having. Here I am; closet drinking, then going to a mental hospital and thinking about suicide, and here he is; about to kill himself through alcohol and drugs and endangering us both via unprotected sex with different women.

And now we were trying to come back together on a spiritual level. We knew we had to find a way to pull this together because we were killing each other, slowly but surely. Our child, Dion, was getting older. The whole time, this child had seen so much of everything that had gone on, not really understanding what was going on. And he now had a brother who visited on the weekends. I knew he was trying to figure all this out. All these events had to have made a major impact on his life.

When you're going through grief or anything like it, it doesn't just impact you; it also has its impacts on everyone around you. If you don't deal with your emotions, if you don't deal with your issues in a productive way, it's going to have an impact on your family. Every decision you make is going to affect someone, but at the time you're going through something, all you can think about is yourself. That's where I was — all I could think about was myself. All I could think about was how I was going to make it through the process. I really wasn't thinking about my whole family's dynamics. I wasn't thinking about how important it was for me to be who I needed to be for my family. I wasn't thinking about the importance of my roles as wife and mother. Mentally, I saw myself in a cave. Nobody else was in this cave but me.

I think this is where the enemy tries to get us. He loves to get us in these dark places so that we can see no one else but ourselves and no one else matters. And we end up abusing ourselves. I abused myself because I internalized so much. I look back at those times when I became the Inspector Gadget ... snooping through Steve's phone and computer, inspecting and researching, staying up all night long to find out clues to the infidelity I already knew was going on. I was driving myself crazy. I spent more energy snooping on him than I did on things more worthy of my time, like working on myself and being a better mother to Dion. There were times that Dion wanted my attention, but I'd say, "Go to bed" or "Go do something else" because I was busy checking up on Steve. I cringe at the state of mind I was in at the time.

If we would just look at the entire situation at times like these, we'd realize what we're getting ourselves into. We'd realize that the enemy is leading us down a dark path and is playing us like little puppets. While he's doing that, he's got our families off on the sidelines, setting *them* up for destruction. Once satan failed to persuade me to kill myself, he devised a strategic plan to get me off focus. It's his job! The Word of God says in John 10:10a that "the thief cometh not but for to steal, and to kill, and to destroy." The enemy's plan for me, when he took my son out, was for me to take myself out. And if I'd taken myself out, Steve might have taken himself out. When these things didn't happen, satan said, "OK, then I'll work on destroying their marriage." He tried as hard as he could to do just that. For a number of years, our marriage had been on a roller-coaster ride of adultery, alcohol and drugs.

I sometimes wondered "Why didn't I leave? Why did I remain in that particular situation?" I found that Pastor Riva Tims — ex-wife of Zachery Tims, the late pastor of the megachurch New Destiny Christian Center in Apopka, Fla. — asked herself the same questions. Zachery Tims, who reportedly had affairs and abused drugs, was found dead inside a New York hotel room on Aug. 12, 2011. Riva Tims discusses their 15-year marriage in her book, *When it All Falls Apart: Find Healing, Joy and Victory through the Pain* (Charisma House), released March 6, 2012.

I have concluded that the reason I stayed with my husband is that I loved Steve. I wanted to see our marriage work. Despite our problems, this was someone that I truly felt I wanted to spend the rest of my life with. When you feel like this about your spouse, you'll do all that you can to make the marriage work. You'll put all the energy you can into making it work. And I trusted God enough to believe that He could restore our marriage.

We thank You, Jehovah Jireh, for those you send to serve as spiritual mentors for us when we need guidance in how to rightly and fully connect with You. We thank You for people who see us through Your eyes and are a tangible manifestation of Your love. We thank You for Your Holy Word, through which you always speak to us. We thank you for the ability, given by your Holy Spirit, to go back to your Word and draw new revelation even from passages we've read time and time again. You have provided us with every tool we need for healing, deliverance, liberty, and relationship restoration. Lord, we praise your holy name ... forever.

Chapter Six

Turnaround
The Burning process?

In 1 Peter 3:1, wives are admonished to minister to ungodly husbands by their conduct: "Likewise, ye wives, be in subjection to your own husbands; that, if any obey not the Word, they also may without the Word be won by the conversation of the wives." I believe my trust in God and His Word was instrumental in Steve's transformation.

Once he went through his brokenness and allowed himself to be ministered to, Steve accepted his call into ministry. He began to work in the church. This was a season in his life, and in our marriage, when things began to flourish again. I compare it to the instance in which farmers, at the end of the season, begin to burn off their harvested fields and till the ground to begin a new crop. The "burning process" in our marriage began and strengthened ... and then, one morning, I got up and realized that my intense pain over Li'l Steve's death just wasn't there anymore.

I could see God getting glory in different areas of my life, which helped me to strengthen my faith. In every situation I could see my faith being increased.

Every time something else came up, I knew God allowed it to happen for a reason and I knew I could make it through. I only needed to say, "God, whatever it is that's going on, You're going to have to show me how to triumph in this situation because right now it hurts and I don't understand it." I would also search His Word for clues on what He might be saying to me.

When my husband saw me searching the Word in every difficult situation, he began to do the same. It's as if he decided, "There must be something about this, because this woman should be broken by now." He came to me one day and said, "I really don't know where you get your strength from. I look at you sometimes and I don't understand. I've got to get that same strength. I've got to find a way to do it so that I won't be in the same situation a year from now." And he started praying with me.

I've always had a prayer area where I'd just come in and pray, sometimes hours at a time, and meditate. He would come in and see that intimacy between God and me. He knew something had shifted, and he wanted a part of it. And this is where I tell people all the time about 1 Peter 3:1. Although my husband was a believer, he still didn't believe ... until he saw the shift in me. It wasn't about what I was doing at church. It wasn't about how I conducted myself around other people. It was about how he saw me in my private, intimate time with God, and how he saw me triumph in challenging situations.

He also saw how I quickly came to his defense if someone said anything negative about our marriage. Imagine me, going from saying hurtful things *to* him to defending and esteeming him to those who would talk *about* him! Before, I couldn't esteem him ... because I didn't know *how* to esteem him in my pain. It's hard to esteem your spouse, or any loved one, who is causing you pain!

But that's exactly what the Spirit of the Lord showed me that I had to do. "*Every* time you feel this pain, begin to esteem your husband," He said.

I thought that was the craziest thing! "Holy Spirit, I don't know what you're talking about," I replied. "This doesn't make any sense to me. I'm hurting, I'm in pain. *He's* hurting me; can you see this?"

"I see all," He responded. "I know all. I know everything that's going on in your life. Everything that's going on in your future, I already know. And I need you to trust Me."

So I began to follow this and other instructions God gave me to minister to my husband. I began to speak life into my marriage. It felt like childbirth to me! When you're in a birthing process, the contractions are coming and you're in a lot of pain, but you're feeling joy at the same time. I felt pain obeying God, but I felt joy too ... even a sense of relief, because I knew that God was going to restore Steve.

Mind you, I still struggled, spiritually. There were still times that I'd be intoxicated even on Sundays when I'd go to church! I wasn't as "muddy" as I was before, but I was not completely clear of the mud.

It's so important to realize that healing doesn't happen overnight. (It's like becoming saved: You don't automatically stop having urges to sin once you have accepted Christ.) People who don't realize this sometimes become discouraged and fall back into destructive lifestyles. Sometimes we, as members of the body of Christ, drive them away by being judgmental of them when they continue to stumble. And they end up missing out on their calling.

Redefining myself, redeveloping myself and restructuring my mindset was work. I had to go through that in-to-me-see process and begin to see Christ in me as well as whom I was in Him. It was a process for me to change my habits, my thoughts, the people I associated with, the way I handled things.

It took time for me to go from drowning my pain with alcohol to wanting a new and better way of life; understanding what it truly meant to be born again; understanding that I had to begin to apply the Scriptures to my life, and then doing just that … reading Scriptures, praying them, putting them into me.

During my process, I discovered I had some mental strongholds even before Li'l Steve's death. One of these was a sense of rejection that I believe stemmed from my leaving my parents' house to live with my grandparents. I think one reason I held onto the pain from Li'l Steve's death for so long was because it gave me the attention I felt I didn't get when I was younger. I think sometimes we begin to manipulate our grief if we don't know how to process it well.

I believe my issues also stemmed from seeing my father struggle with drugs and alcohol for those many years. I cannot remember a time in my childhood that he did not have this struggle. I know I brought a lot of my dysfunctional family dynamics to my marriage. When you haven't known anything *but* a dysfunctional lifestyle, you're subjected to thinking its normal, or dismissing it because you've dealt with worse dysfunction! That explains why I held onto my marriage despite its dysfunction. I was a magnet for dysfunction, because that's all I knew! I didn't know what a healthy marriage was like, because I wasn't raised within one. So when my marriage became troubled, I had no point of comparison. Becoming intimate with myself —

my in-to-me-see — revealed so many ugly things resulting from my sense of worthlessness and sense of rejection.

I'd seen my father deal with his problems for many years by drinking, so I decided to drink. I'm thankful I didn't get into drugs. I have family members who have gone that route because they felt it was the only route they could take. That's why I can sympathize with those who have been around substance abuse all their lives and have therefore fallen into that same trap. It's a generational curse.

When I was at that crossroads, I could have decided to continue the substance abuse. But I chose to follow God. He gives us so many signs — especially "yield" signs and warning signs! Sometimes those signs are in neon! He sounds the alarm, lowers the crossing arms. But oftentimes, we ignore the Holy Spirit. I ignored the Holy Spirit many times. The enemy wanted me to drown myself in alcohol because I wouldn't be able to hear God in that state.

Talking through my problems with Granny Rose enabled me to clear my mind up, and despite my continuing taste for alcohol, I continued to work toward my healing. This is what anybody who faced what I faced has to understand: They must continue to work; to fight and to keep going. Even if they don't put the bottle down the first week, even if they don't put the bottle down the second week ... they must continue to keep going in the right direction.

Trying to walk in other directions had gotten me to a point of spiritual exhaustion. I couldn't find solace anywhere. You know what they say about hitting rock bottom — there's nowhere else to go but up. I'd gotten to the point where the only thing I wanted to find out was what was in God's Word. So I got down on the floor and began to study the Word. I absorbed all the Scriptures I could, and began to listen to tapes of different Bible teachings. I also continued my sessions with Granny Rose.

Gradually, my life began taking a shift. I can't pinpoint an exact time that I stopped drinking; all I can say is that one day, I didn't have that urge to go to the liquor store anymore. That next drink didn't matter to me anymore. It didn't matter to me what Steve might be doing wrong ... or what anyone else might have been doing wrong. All that mattered to me was being filled with the Holy Spirit. I wanted to learn more about God. I wanted to walk in His path.

This is why it was easier to forgive my husband. I'd come to the full realization of the forgiveness and grace I needed, and had received, from God as well as awareness and an understanding of the attacks of the enemy.

Steve began to see the shift in me. (Although he may not have known the extent of my drinking, he knew I was covering my pain with alcohol.) As he began to see the shift in me, he began to ask questions. He began to want a shift in his own life. And as God began to shift and restore him, Steve began to fall in love with God as he never had before.

El-Shaddai, Many-breasted One, God of the Impossible ... we know that you can make a way where there is no way! We know that you can raise anything from the dead — whether it be dead people or dead marriages and relationships, and whether the dead be physically dead or spiritually dead. Right now in the name of Jesus, we ask that you resurrect and restore anything in our lives that you meant to live, but which we have allowed to die ... especially our Christian witness and our Christian walk. We thank You for your patience as we work toward manifesting in the natural what You have already done in the spirit. In the sweet name of Jesus our Lord, Amen.

Chapter Seven

Just Like My Own

I came to love Terrance. I looked at him one day during one of the weekends he'd come to visit, and I realized that I felt the same love for him that I felt for Dion. I looked at Terrance and saw him looking like my husband. I saw Steve's seed. This moment of realization helped me to understand the Old Testament story of sisters Rachel and Leah, both wives of Jacob, both mothers of his children. Terrance's mother and I were not biological sisters. But we were both children of God, and I realized how important it was for me not to harbor anger toward her. I was able to love her child as if her child was my child.

When Steve first told me I would have to accept Terrance, I did so for the wrong reason: I wanted to remain married to Steve. But accepting Terrance was one thing; loving him was another, and Terrance deserved to be loved.

"You love him because I love him," God told me. "You love him because I love *you*."

I'm reminded of the Biblical story of Ishmael (Gen. 16-17), the first son of Abraham, born because Abraham's wife Sarah (instead of trusting God) told Abraham to sleep with her handmaid, Hagar, in order to have a child. In so many words, God told Abraham, "Even though Ishmael was not part of the promise I made to you, I will bless him." Every soul is important to God. So I had to love Terrance with the love of God. It had nothing to do with my husband; nothing to do with Terrance's mother; nothing to do with anyone else. It had everything to do with God and His love. That way, I could love Terrance unconditionally.

Prior to this, I felt shame in being out in public with him. People who knew us would ask, "Who is this child? Wait a minute; this boy looks like he's not too far from Dion in age." Then they'd start to put two and two together. And church people? They will hurt you more than anybody! Here I was, taking three little boys to church — Steve's firstborn Kedric, who was 6 months old when his father and I first met; then Dion and Terrance. Not only was I questioned, the children were, too! "Is this your brother?" they'd ask Dion. "Where'd he come from? Who is his mama?" At the time, I didn't know how to deal with that. When people asked questions, I would become offended. How fast we become offended when our back is up against a wall! I'd also feel anger toward Steve because I felt he'd put me in an embarrassing situation — being made to feel as though I had to explain his actions.

But once I began to understand that the enemy was trying to destroy me and that God wanted to do something different in this, I began to let that anger go. My husband could see that I was letting it go.

My healing continued, and the new me blossomed. Steve's unfaithfulness, and its consequences, were no longer things I was magnifying. I could look back and say "OK, it was hurting real bad at that time but it doesn't hurt like it used to. I have the scar, but it doesn't hurt the same way anymore." Not only did it not hurt the same way, but now I could understand that in my struggle was a message for someone else. I was not proud of what happened, but I understand how God got the glory out of it.

By now Dion and Kedric were forming a bond with their brother. The boys were spending weekends together. My stepson and Dion wanted to know when their brother was coming over, when they were going to go do this and when they were going to do that. I realized that this situation went far beyond Steve and me. So I began to communicate with Terrance's mother, asking when he was going to come over, asking what he needed. At the time I found out about her, I'd thought, *How pitiful on your part that you would put yourself into this position.* And I downplayed her. Now, here I was, doing something I never thought I would do: building a relationship with her. Yes, it hurt in the beginning. Yes, I had to process that pain. Yes, I had to conquer those same feelings of anger and resentment and bitterness that built up after Li'l Steve's death. Yes, I had to overcome going back down that slippery slope. Thank God, I did.

I really think people need to see this type of situation from a perspective other than their own. Seeing it through God's eyes helped me to understand it clearly. When Terrance's mother first came to drop him off, I put on a front, pretending that my household was fine. In the beginning, neither of us let the other know how she felt. But there came a time that I started to feel the sorrow of God for her. Here this woman was, a single mother, raising a child she had by a married man. Here was a woman who had been manipulated from the beginning. I figured she had the same low self-esteem, the same insecurities, as other women who fall into traps like this. She'd believed Steve when he told her he was going through a divorce. She'd believed the relationship had a future. In the end, she had to have felt lonely and betrayed. I was sure she'd mentally kicked herself: *Here I am having his child and he's still with his wife. How foolish I was! How childish of me to get myself into this situation*! (It wasn't until years later that she confided in me, confirming what I'd seen when I looked at her through spiritual eyes.)

So I began to find ways I could accommodate her as a mother. Everything I did for Dion or Kedric, I would do for Terrance. On the weekends, I would make sure he was picked up. If Steve didn't go get him, I would go get him. Dion played baseball, so I would always make sure the boys were at the baseball games together. I wanted them to be raised together. And I realized that it didn't matter *how* things had come to be. They were brothers and I wanted them to be close to each other. I always told them, "Never let people try to divide you into 'stepbrothers' or 'half-brothers.' You guys are brothers." To this day I tell Kedric and Terrance, "You're my sons." They call me Mama Tiffany because I've always been mom to the three of them.

Looking into me, finding out who I really was, dealing with those issues I had and healing from them, helped me to be able to love like this.

Regardless of all the things that had gone on, I could see God's plan to use me as another mother figure for Terrance. I made an impact on his life because he spent time with me. When I realized that I had to capitalize on that and not allow the enemy to destroy our relationship, I treated him with love and kindness. When he came to me, he knew he was secure in my presence. He felt secure in my arms because I was his mother. When people saw me with the boys, they could never distinguish between my biological son and my non-biological sons. They were, and are, very much my sons.

And when Steve saw me love on Terence unconditionally, he was like, "Wow. There's something about this woman." It was this situation, also, that prompted Steve to begin to talk about wanting to restore our marriage, wanting to be healed, wanting to get what I was receiving, wanting to know how to get there.

One night he came to me in the bedroom and he just began to cry.

"Tiffany, I know I've made a lot of mistakes," he said "I know I've messed up. I don't know how to stop doing some of the things I'm doing. I don't know how to do this on my own; I know I'm a mess. And the only thing that's going to help me is if you walk me through and help me through this process."

I knew he was crying out to me; I just didn't know how to help. I was like that person who is learning how to ride a bike. He wants his friends to ride with him, but his friends can't ride, and he doesn't know how to show them because he is still learning himself. I wasn't strong enough to help Steve at this point, and I realized that. I could pray him through, but I couldn't help him on my own.

So I went to Granny Rose and told her about our conversation. On her advice, we sought counseling with someone outside our church. And that's how we began to put our marriage back together.

Things were going so very well. I could see Steve's and my love being restored, the passion being restored, the intimacy being restored. Once again, I saw the person I fell in love with when we were 17 years old.

He told me he knew that our marriage was going to be used to heal people. At the time I couldn't see it. I knew we were on the road to recovery, but I couldn't see how anybody would want to listen to two people like us. *We are a mess!* I thought. *Why would anybody want to listen to us?* (Of course the enemy tries to overcome us with shame and guilt so that we don't want to give our testimony.) I told Steve, "I don't know how God is going to do that, but if that's what you're saying God is going to do, we'll believe God for that."

We were still very immature in the Word, very immature as Christians. Although we had been raised in the church, we didn't know a lot about the Word of God. We were just trying to hang on to the few Scriptures we knew, trying to rebuild ourselves and rebuild our marriage.

But our spiritual maturity grew. We became so strong in the church, it became noticeable to others. Proverbs 18:16 says, "A man's gift maketh room for him, and bringeth him before great men." As God began to make room for our gifts then our gifts made room for us. People wanted to hear our testimony. Granted, some may have wanted to hear us because they were simply nosy. But many of our listeners just wanted to receive a healing. God was using us mightily. We were praying for people, sitting in marriage groups, counseling other couples. I felt so excited about what God was doing with our marriage. I could see why He had restored it and was showing us how to reveal our love languages again.

And as I developed an even deeper desire for God, I realized there was a call on my life. So I went to ministry school and became a licensed minister. I began to minister in different places. At the same time, God was strengthening me in the Word. I gained knowledge of His Word like never before. It was like I was reading the pages, and all of a sudden I would feel his Word illuminate me from within. My spiritual ears became sensitive. God would warn me of something and I would hear, and heed, His warning. Or I would study a particular Scripture for weeks, then all of a sudden something would happen and I would find myself able to apply that Scripture to that situation. God was building me up. He was building our family up — things were changing for the better in Dion's life as well.

God's Word is necessary in his redefinition of us. The enemy goes away only for a season. We must lay hold of every Scripture God reveals to us, because there's going to come a time when we're going to need that particular Scripture. Take note of it — it's for a purpose.

Father God, please help us to forgive as You forgive, and love as You love. Help us to forgive and love when our flesh screams that it's impossible! Remind us of Romans 5:8 — that "[You] commendeth [Your] love toward us, in that, while we were yet sinners, Christ died for us." Help us to remember that loving others despite natural odds is a reward in itself: We become a reflection of Your glory. In His name, Amen.

Chapter Eight

Back Down the Slippery Slope

Ministering together, my husband and I soon built a reputation as a power couple. We'd been through the storm. We'd lost our child. We'd overcome infidelity, alcohol and drug abuse, and here we were, counseling and doing marriage conferences and seminars all over the city.

We became so strong that the enemy just couldn't take it. He launched another attack.

God showed me, through a vision, what was going to happen: A woman was going to come into our church and tempt Steve. He showed me the woman. I tried to warn Steve, but he thought I was still holding onto unforgiveness over his past actions.

"No, I'm trying to warn you that this is going to happen," I insisted. But he didn't receive this from me.

God, good as He is, sent someone else, a brother in Christ, to give Steve the exact same warning.

"I see this woman," the brother told him. "You're going to be overtaken by this, because you're going to be flattered by the attention — by what you *think* the person wants from you. But this is the enemy coming to destroy the anointing that's on your life. He's going to *start* with you, because he has to attack the head first. Once he attacks the head, he can scatter your family."

Steve refused to receive that warning, too.

God used another person to warn him a third time, laying out a similar scenario. Again, he refused to heed it.

It was six months or so later when it happened. (When satan sees your attention is off him is when he will send his agent into your camp.) The woman came to the church. She seemed to be someone who would never do anything like this ... which made her the perfect weapon of the enemy. She began to show my husband attention. That same old spirit began to rise up and reattach itself to him. He began to snowball. When he got to a certain point, I told him, "I see what is going on." But he was too embarrassed and ashamed to admit he was caught up again.

People must understand the importance of acknowledging a sin at its very onset. If you acknowledge the work of the enemy at the very onset and repent, your heart will not become hardened to the sin. But Steve didn't acknowledge his sin; nor did he repent. He continued to allow himself to play in that ground.

My husband had never been to theology school or seminary. But the Lord had given him the anointing to be able to articulate the Word of God with power. People couldn't believe how much knowledge he had received! This man had been drinking, smoking, and some of everything else just a few years earlier. He went through such a fast, progressive anointing process that when it came to full fruition, it was unbelievable. God had redeemed the time. Steve himself was astonished, let alone everyone who heard him express the knowledge God had given him to rightly divide His Word. We were all in awe, because we knew it was God.

The enemy's attacks can be fast, too, as well as subtle. Steve allowed himself to get in deeper and deeper into his backslidden state. He went from that first woman to the next woman to the next woman — back to back to back. The infidelity was much worse than it had been the first time. He began to look and sound like a totally different person.

Steve was so demonically overtaken; he thought everyone who came to him wanted him. He was convinced that I was going to reject him. I tried to talk to him. "Steve, you've got to see this; I'm not trying to leave," I told him. "I'm trying to help you through this. We're going to fight through this; we're going to work through this." He even saw *this* as a direct attack. He thought I was after his anointing.

I kept trying to get through to him nonetheless, knowing that we were greater together than we were apart. But he just became more convinced that I — along with anyone who warned him about his actions, including friends, his aunts, even his own mother — was attacking him.

Steve got so out of control that the Lord began to openly expose what he'd been doing in secret. God Himself was yet trying to warn him, trying to get him out of the situation he was in. But he would not take heed.

Once the enemy had regained a foothold in Steve's life, he began to attack the rest of us. Again, when he attacks the head, the body is vulnerable. Eventually, after trying in vain to warn him, I became frustrated. My frustration and my hurt made me angry once again. So I found myself back in that same dark place I vowed I would never revisit. I was so devastated; I just wanted Steve out of the space. I felt uneasy walking into my house because my household was under such a vicious demonic attack. Granny Rose felt it too. She came over for a family gathering and told me, "I'm not comfortable in this house."

There was no peace. If Steve was being attacked, and I was being attacked, of course my son was being attacked; more on that later.

In Matthew 12 and Luke 11, Jesus told a parable about an unclean spirit coming back with a vengeance — and with some mean company — if allowed to re-enter a territory. In Matthew 12:43-45, He says:

> **When the unclean spirit is gone out of a man, he walketh through dry places, seeking rest, and findeth none. Then he saith, I will return into my house from whence I came out; and when he is come, he findeth it empty, swept, and garnished. Then goeth he, and taketh with himself seven other spirits more wicked than himself, and they enter in and dwell there: and the last state of that man is worse than the first. Even so shall it be also unto this wicked generation.**

Here we all were, in this house whose atmosphere felt just like what Jesus described in that parable. Here Steve and I were both still in the church, both still doing ministry, both living this lie.

I'm sure there are many couples in the body of Christ who are experiencing this problem now and don't know how to seek deliverance by combating the enemy the way they're supposed to ... together. There was no "together" in our case; in fact, when

I began to see my husband move toward this other woman who came to our church, I knew I had lost him completely. I knew that he loved me because of who I was to him and the years we had together and the things we experienced together. But he was no longer *in love with me.* A woman knows these things; she just knows.

Things only got worse. Steve had been diagnosed with post-traumatic stress disorder too and had begun to go to the Veterans Administration Hospital for counseling. "I think we need to contact your counselor and speak with him, because not only are you dealing with some spiritual things, you're also dealing with some mental issues," I told him.

Steve did speak to his counselor, which resulted in him being put on a different type of medication. The spiritual issues were still not being addressed ... and you cannot medicate spiritual issues. The Web definition of "spiritual" is "of, relating to, or affecting the human spirit or soul as opposed to material or physical things," while the Web definition of "mental" is "of or relating to the mind." He was trying to drown out the spiritual issues instead of dealing with them spiritually.

When Steve went back into infidelity, I began to feel as though I couldn't win. I was vulnerable, and vulnerability is one of those things the enemy uses to his advantage. I believe infidelity is one of those cases in which the person being cheated on is subject to feel as though the situation is his or her fault. In the past, it had been easy to blame my grief over Li'l Steve. Now, I was beginning to feel that something about me must have caused Steve to fall out of love with me. And in my vulnerable state, it was easy for me to listen to some other man say things to me — "You're pretty," or "You look very attractive." So when someone else DID begin to compliment me, I was flattered. After all, I wasn't hearing these things from Steve.

At the time, it seemed strange that someone with Steve's and my level of maturity would still be played by the enemy and lose so much ground. I can see now, though, that it's easy for those who seem the strongest — especially those in ministry and leadership — to fall prey to these attacks. Many don't want to admit it.

At any rate, satan was sending these flattering men my way. I begin to think, *OK, well, maybe there's something different out here for me.* I reasoned that since Steve had turned to other women, I had to have somebody. It was the old "if you can't beat 'em, join' em" mentality. At one point I entertained conversations with several different men via text messaging and phone calls.

One thing I'll make clear: It's really easy to find fault in someone else when you seem to be "right", but when you find yourself in that same situation you tend to have more compassion for the one you condemned. Although some of my actions may not have taken me down some of the paths Steve may have taken, the fact is that I was still wrong, because I became emotionally connected to the other men. In Matthew 5:27-28, Jesus, during his Sermon on the Mount, said, "Ye have heard that it was said by them of old time, Thou shalt not commit adultery: But I say unto you, That whosoever looketh on a woman to lust after her hath committed adultery with her already in his heart." That's a powerful admonition for both sexes today — and texts and phone conversations can certainly be seen as more than just "looking."

I became caught up with one man in particular, a man who brought up the possibility of my getting a divorce from Steve and marrying him. We discussed this scenario and created this whole fantasy life together, all through phone calls and texts. I also found myself sharing with him intimate details about my family, my marriage, things going on in my household and other business. (Ultimately, this relationship ended when God moved this man out of state. Once he was gone, our conversations became more and more infrequent, then ceased altogether.) Funny how God will save you from your own madness. This situation could've gone much crazier had God not removed this individual from around me. It may seem strange but when you become emotionally connected to someone other than your spouse; you have already committed adultery. I am not proud to admit this; but I know it is necessary for my freedom and for others who are going through the same thing to realize having an emotional, intimate connection with anyone other than your spouse is nothing short of adultery.

At this point, Dion was in his mid-teens and very aware of the romantic relationships that develop between men and women. He was also very aware of the change of atmosphere between my husband and me. There were times that I'd be texting or on the phone, having an inappropriate conversation. Once, Dion looked on my phone and saw the number of a man Steve knew.

"Why was he calling you?" Dion asked.

"Oh, he was just looking for your daddy," I lied.

I couldn't get rid of Dion that easily. "No — why is he calling YOUR number instead of calling HIS number?"

I lied again. "Well, he must have called Steve's number and couldn't get him, so now he's calling my number, trying to find him."

My son is very smart ... and he knew very well why the phone call was coming in. He was looking at me like, "Here's my mom right in the same boat with my daddy." Now I had this confused child trying to figure out what was going on between his parents.

For many years he had seen his father engaging in infidelity, but never had he seen his mom in this situation. Never had he seen me battling this particular spirit.

I think the only thing that made me feel an ounce of guilt *was* the fact that Dion knew what I was up to. It hurt for him to see me in that light. (I should ultimately have been ashamed of the fact that *God* saw me once again dealing with my pain in the wrong way. Although I felt guilt, I didn't feel it for the primary reason I should have felt it.)

But one day, while in the bathtub, I began praying. "God, why am I yearning to talk to this person and be in his presence when he isn't even my husband? This is not of You, God. I *know* this is not of You." I began to ask for forgiveness.

I realized that once again, I'd gotten to a place where I didn't even care what my husband was doing. I had gone back to what was familiar, but in a different format: Whereas, I had used alcohol to dull my pain before, I used another man to dull it this time. The enemy doesn't care how he gets us... he just wants us back in his trap.

While I was still trying to sort through all this, Steve and I had a big argument. He'd seen the text messages, too, and started confronting me about the relationship he knew I was having with this other guy. Dion, now 15, witnessed the argument, which got completely out of control, and became angry. He got in the middle of the fight with his own outburst, revealing things he had been told about us by some people at school who knew my husband. Afterward, Dion left and went to stay with my mom for what turned out to be two weeks.

"I think it's best that we let him stay where he is, because right now, we are both a mess," I told Steve. "We are doing nothing but damaging him. We just all need to calm down and come back together again and then try to talk from there."

Steve was having issues, I was having issues, and our son was caught in the middle. That's when we both decided we needed to get some family counseling. But during the counseling sessions, Steve and I were never on one accord. We were both too busy trying to point fingers at each other. I would say, "Yeah, I'm wrong but if you wouldn't have ...," and he would say, "Yeah, I'm wrong but if you remember when ...." It was just so much compounded mess.

When Steve and I had received counseling as a couple before, we had both able to come to a common ground and say to each other, "I'm going to humble myself and submit to the fact that I hurt you and you hurt me. And we're going to work through this. I love you enough to work through this." This time, the marriage had not just been badly bent; it was broken. We should have said to each other, "I'm going to pull off my mask and you pull off yours and let's work this out together — as ugly as it may be, and as devastating as it may be to each of us." But during these several counseling sessions, which were more like battles, we both went in with a mind-set of self-preservation.

And there was Dion, 16 by now, not understanding any of it. During counseling, he basically shut down. Looking at things from his perspective, I realize this all must have been devastating for him. He had tried to figure this situation out, and he couldn't do it. He didn't understand all of the dynamics of my grief over Li'l Steve, because he'd been an infant then. He had to grow up in the midst of all this grief, not understanding where it was coming from. He had to witness infidelity in his parents' marriage, and the child that resulted. He saw us enjoying a few golden years as a result of our healing; he saw the burst of spiritual energy that resulted in our combined ministry. And now, he was seeing us back in the same valley we'd been delivered from ... only this time with both Steve *and* me carrying on with people outside our marriage and neither of us humbling ourselves.

Dear Lord, please sharpen us in the spirit to always take Your divine warnings seriously. Grant us the gift of discernment so that when the enemy comes to tempt us, we will not be taken unawares. Help us to be like the 300 members of Gideon's army, who in Judges 7 passed Your test by remaining watchful of their surroundings as they cupped their hands to drink water. Help us to be open, humble and teachable so that neither pride nor shame will get in the way of our correcting any ungodly behavior brought to our attention by our sisters and brothers. We ask this in the name of the Lord Jesus, our Lion of Judah and kinsman-redeemer. Amen.

Chapter Nine

Tribulation and Restoration

It's simple, really, how the enemy works to destroy marriages. It's a wonder we keep falling for it! Division comes in when one doesn't want to submit to the other. The Apostle Paul, in Ephesians 5:21, told married couples that they should be "submitting yourselves one to another in the fear of God." When there is no submission and no humility, the marriage is doomed.

And a 16-year-old preacher's son who's seeing one thing outside of the home and another in the home can easily conclude, "This God thing isn't working for me because I don't see it working for my parents." Because Steve and I were unwilling to submit to each other, satan had a clear path to attack our son.

Prior to this, Dion had been a very active, outgoing boy, having played baseball since he was 4 years old. But with our mess taking a toll on him, he stopped eating and became sullen and uncommunicative. He began to skip classes and act out at school, getting into fights. He started hanging out with the wrong crowd and smoking marijuana, and then he graduated to prescription drugs he'd gotten on the street.

When I started to notice this change in Dion's behavior, Steve and I began to get into arguments about him.

"Something's not right," I'd say.

"Leave him alone," Steve said. "You've been nagging me; now you want to nag him."

We couldn't even come together on getting help for our son.

Now there was total disagreement in every aspect of our marriage and our household. When I got off from work, my stomach would get into knots driving home because I knew there'd be some upsetting issue waiting for me. There were times I didn't even want to *go* home; it was that bad.

Still, we were going to church every Sunday. Still, we were sitting there in the sanctuary, all smiles, shouting "Hallelujah, thank you Jesus." After service was over, we'd go right back to the same stinky situation we'd left at home.

Finally, there was an incident that required us to seek intervention with Dion. While at the mall with some friends, he was arrested for shoplifting. We had to go to juvenile court. Steve and I were ordered to go through a series of counseling sessions with Dion.

As we went through these sessions, Dion became even more rebellious. He felt we were actually trying to hurt him by consenting to allow the juvenile justice system to do what we were supposed to be doing as parents. He began to act out even more. Whenever I'd come to Steve about a Dion-related issue that had arisen, he would respond, "Tiff, leave him alone. You're putting too much pressure on him. You're expecting too much out of him." In a misguided attempt to help Dion, Steve was siding with him, trying to be his friend rather than a parent.

So, in trying to save our son, I was at odds with my husband more than ever. If we could not be a united force as husband and wife, we definitely couldn't stand together as parents. Dion now knew he could go to his dad about certain things instead of coming to both of us. Now he had leverage to manipulate us in order to get away with whatever he wanted to get away with.

Eventually Steve's attempt to be buddies with Dion fell apart, too. Now Dion knew things about Steve ... things Dion was hearing, seeing, even getting involved with. Whenever he became angry with Steve, he would say, "Well, yeah, Dad, why don't you tell Mom about so and so?"

Dion had transformed into someone I knew he wasn't. And this, too, had happened fast.

Right after the shoplifting incident at the mall, Dion seemed to fall deeper and deeper into depression. His education continued to suffer. In one year, he attended three different high schools. I had to get him out of North Pulaski High School, where he'd attended the previous year, and put him in Mills University Studies High School. He began getting into more trouble at Mills, so I withdrew him and put him into eStem Public Charter Schools. Then I moved him to Robinson High School. Seeing him sinking deeper, I was doing everything I could do to save him.

And getting Dion back and forth to Robinson was a chore. The school is located far out on Highway 10 in west Little Rock ... a long way from our home in the far southeastern end of North Little Rock. I'd drop him off in the morning before work, then that afternoon I would leave my office in downtown Little Rock to pick him up, bring him back to work, and finish my duties for the day before heading home with him. I did this for almost the entire 2011-2012 school year.

Ironically, since his attempt to "buddy up" with Dion had backfired, Steve began to get angry at me for doing all this. "Steve I see that he's being rebellious," I told him. "But we have to admit that he's not in this place on his own. We've had some part in this." I suggested that since Dion was having so many issues in the public school system, perhaps we should pull him out altogether and home-school him. Steve disagreed. I don't even know why I thought we would come to an agreement on that.

As it turned out, my attempts to save Dion were all for nothing. I thought Robinson school would be better for him, but things only got worse. And he was skipping school anyway. After I dropped him off there, somebody would pick him up and he would leave campus. I was getting calls from the principal every other day.

Everything I'd tried had failed. I felt so helpless and hopeless. Trying to save my son from disaster seemed to be propelling him toward it even faster, having a more negative impact. And the marriage continued to worsen. Steve was on one side of the house and I was on the other.

"Dion, why don't we just take you out of school a year and take you to California?" I'd asked him before the school year started. My uncle lived in California and I wanted Dion to get around someone who would be a positive influence and help him find his ground. But he balked at the idea because of his girlfriend. They'd been seeing each other for a couple of years and he was so in love with her, he did not want to leave Arkansas.

When he was about to turn 18, Dion decided he was going to drop out of school and move out. "You guys can't tell me what to do anymore," he told us. "I'm grown now and I'm going to find my way because what y'all have going on isn't the right way. So since you guys don't know the right way, I'll go and find out the right way myself. I'm not going to stay here in this house, because everything here ain't the truth anyway. It's nothing but a big lie and I'm tired of living this big lie." (I later had to look at myself in the mirror one day and say, "If this child can sit here and tell you he's tired of living this big lie, when will YOU be tired of living it?")

Dion left to go stay with my mom again. I remember coming to the conclusion that it was simply over between Steve and me. We had taken that marriage as far as it could go.

Let me say here that I really should have left, prior to all this happening. You see, God had released me from the marriage after Steve gave in to temptation with the woman he'd been warned about. I'm reminded of that incident in 1 Samuel 15 where King Saul started down his own spiritual slippery slope. God, through Samuel, had told Saul to destroy *all the Amelekites — and everything they had* — while defeating them in battle. Instead, Saul spared the Amelekite King, Agag, and saved the best of the livestock. God took the anointing from Saul. In Chapter 16, He told Samuel, "Don't even cry over him anymore! I've chosen another man to be king. Get up and go to Jesse's house and get ready to anoint a new king. I'll tell you who he is."

I had stayed in the marriage, however, out of concern over what people would say and what toll our split would take on those to whom we had ministered. I was actually told by several people in the church how important it was for us to stay together because so many others were looking at us. I didn't want to be the cause of people saying, "I saw so much hope in your marriage. I saw so much hope in you. And now you are divorced. How can you minister hope and restoration to someone?" So often those of us in ministry take hits, for the sake of the people, that God didn't intend for us to take.

And, as it happened, the person who depended on me the most was the person I let down. It was almost like I chose the people over giving my son a healthy environment. I tried to fix what God had already told me was over and done, and when I couldn't fix it, I fell back into the pit, this time, pulling Dion in with me. I suffered great repercussions for holding on to the marriage.

I know many people will wonder, "How was that of God — that He would desire for you to be divorced?" It was God's will for us to remain married. But it was *Steve's and my* will to leave the path, and God gave us free will. Often, people remain in dead marriages, or other dead situations, because they are stuck on this traditional religious doctrine that frustrates the grace of God. God does not mean for us to remain in situations that are going to kill us, physically or spiritually.

In October 2012, right after he turned 18, Dion had a big falling out with Steve. He'd run into Steve's mistress's children, with whom he just happened to have attended school earlier. "Your dad and my mom have been together for 10 years," he was told. This is how your deeds always find you out!

Dion didn't want to believe it. He came home really upset. "Mom, I've got something to tell you," he said. "I'm mad, but I know you're going to tell Dad, so I'm just going to wait until he gets here ... and I'm just going to tell him to his face why I'm mad."

Sure enough, when Steve got home, Dion confronted him. Steve tried to deny everything. "You're lying," Dion said. "I know you're lying, because they know too much about my mama, too much about our family, too much about us and everything about you. And they even call you 'Daddy.'" They got into an argument that ended with Dion leaving to stay with my mom again. I had never seen him so angry, I was scared too.

I called and called Dion that night, but he wouldn't answer his cell phone. The next day, he still wouldn't answer. My mom called me and said, "Oh, he's OK.

He's over here. Just leave him alone for a few days. He'll cool off."

But that next night, my spirit was troubled. I just couldn't sleep. I tossed and turned. Finally I got up and texted Dion: *Don't do anything stupid out of anger. Doing something stupid is not going to change this situation. Please, Dion, listen to me. Don't act out on your anger.*

He didn't respond.

The next morning, Dion called me, crying. "Mom, please come get me out of jail," he pleaded.

"Dion, what are you doing in jail?" I asked, anguished.

He just kept saying over and over, "I didn't do it. I promise you I didn't do it."

"What do they have you locked up for?" I asked again.

"They said I robbed somebody. But Mama, I didn't do it. I promise I didn't do it."

"Dion, they don't have you in jail for no reason," I responded.

As it happened, Dion was with several other young men during a robbery in the River Market District; however, Dion was the only one caught.

I just lost it, because at this point I knew we were about to go through some major issues.

I told Steve, who said, "Well, he's finally done it." He didn't say much else.

I started calling around trying to figure out what was going on. I was naïve not only about the charges Dion faced, but about the adult justice system. I called bail bondsmen to see if I could get him bonded out; of course that was going to cost thousands of dollars. And of course Steve and I were in disagreement once again. "Let him stay locked up," he said.

We did so for several days. I was scared and miserable, not knowing what was going on with him. He had never been away like that before. A citation for shoplifting at the mall when one is a juvenile is one thing. But four adult charges of aggravated robbery is another. And where did he get a weapon from?

After a few days, when Steve saw what a toll the matter was taking on me, he got somebody to get our son bonded out.

Dion came home still insisting that he didn't do it. He was not the person who had produced the weapon, he said. That really didn't matter: If you're there with the "real" perpetrator, you are an accessory to the crime. And he's the only one who got caught; therefore he was the only one who was charged.

I began researching these charges ... and began to realize how much trouble Dion was in. My stomach was in knots. I was a nervous wreck every day. Dion was getting scared and even more depressed with the realization that he's made a huge mistake. He was an 18-year-old kid who wanted to be grown and who'd acted out of his anger.

Things moved fast. We retained an attorney and of course, with charges like that, the attorney's fee was money we didn't have. We were trying to figure out what we would do.

What Steve did, a few weeks after all this happened, was move out. He decided he couldn't remain in the marriage anymore.

I was at work when I got a phone call from Dion. He said "Mama, you need to come home."

I said, "Why?"

"Dad's moving his stuff out."

"What?"

"Yeah, he's moving his stuff out."

"In the middle of the day?"

"Yeah."

I ran into my boss's office and told her I needed to leave due to an emergency at home.

I got home and by this time, Steve was turning the corner from our street. He had his belongings loaded in the back of a truck. Someone else was trailing him in another truck with more items.

I asked, "Steve, what are you doing?"

"I'm leaving," he said.

"You're leaving?"

"Yes."

"Why are you leaving like this?

"Because I'm done."

"Can you come back to the house and we talk?" I asked.

He turned around and followed me back home, only to ask, "What do you want, Tiff?"

"I want to talk," I told him. "I want to find out what's going on. Why are you leaving?"

"I'm leaving because I can't do this anymore. I'm done. I just can't do it anymore."

"So you're saying you're just leaving the marriage? It's over?"

"It's over."

I begged him to stay. I was, in fact, on my knees, crying. "Let's talk. Let's try to resolve this. Let's try to figure out what's going on," I pleaded. "Can we talk this out?" Dion stood behind me, also crying and pleading with *me*: "Mom, why are you even begging? Don't do this to yourself. You don't deserve this."

Steve was not moved. "No, I'm done. I'm out," he replied.

And he left.

I was devastated once again. The problem wasn't so much that he left — I'd realized earlier that our marriage was over. I realized that things had gotten so bad, he didn't want to be there anymore. But the timing of his departure made me feel like I was being kicked while I was down. Now Dion felt neglected and pulled apart ... and we both felt abandoned.

A month after Steve left, I had another rude awakening, this one concerning our finances. Because Steve had pretty much handled the bills, I didn't realize that we were behind in home mortgage payments ... and facing foreclosure. So I found myself fighting for my house — along with trying to figure out how to pay an attorney single-handedly, praying for my son's life, and still trying to trust God in the process. I ultimately decided to pick up a second job to pay for Dion's legal fees.

Dion, facing the prospect of prison, continued to go deeper and deeper into depression. And at this point I just existed. I was so hurt and angry. Once again, that anger was directed above: *God? You know … really? Why would I even trust You anymore? I've lost everything. My husband is gone. My son is facing prison. I'm about to lose my home.*

I just wanted to give up … I didn't even care if I woke up the next day. I hadn't felt like that since Li'l Steve died.

I secluded myself. I wasn't in church anywhere. I wasn't ministering. I completely shut down. I would leave my nine-to-five job, go to the second job, work until 10:30 or 11 o'clock at night, and then go home. I should have been spending quality time with my son, unsure as I was of his future. But I was away for as long as 14 hours a day, depressed, while he sat at home, depressed. (His girlfriend did everything she could to try to console him, but there was only so much she could do.) When I was home, I'd wonder whether I'd hear a knock on my door by bank officials telling me we needed to get out. I was doing all I could to get a loan modification approved, but wasn't getting anywhere. I had no idea how I was going to make it out of this.

Then on Sept. 11, 2013 — nearly a year after Steve left — I received some news that shook me to my core. It came via a phone call one morning somewhere between 3 and 4 a.m. I saw that the call was coming from Steve's phone. I answered, wondering why he was calling me this time in the morning.

"Hello," I said.

I heard a woman's voice. "Tiffany?"

"Yes."

"Tiffany, you don't know me, but I'm calling you to tell you that Steve has passed."

You would think that after being neglected and abandoned, going through all the financial turmoil I had gone through, and dealing with everything Dion was going through — I wouldn't have been hit so hard by the news of Steve's passing. But not only was it devastating as far as *what* happened; *how* I found out the news was especially gut-wrenching. Rather than Steve's mom or other relatives, here was another woman calling to tell me my husband had passed on. This woman was apparently the one who was with Steve at the time of this death. I'd heard he was in a relationship. That didn't hurt me like it had when we lived as husband and wife, but needless to say, I didn't want to get this type of phone call from another woman.

I got myself together and went to the hospital to find out details of Steve's death. His family was there, but the woman who'd called me wasn't. No one really knew anything other than the fact that Steve had passed in his sleep. Now I felt I was truly by myself. This was definitely one of the worst days of my life. The man I had loved for over 20 years was gone; and despite all of our differences I truly loved this man. I never imaged that he would leave this earth so soon. Not to mention the timing of his death and our unresolved issues and disconnect from each other for over a year left me empty and devastated.

I had to gather the strength to call Dion and tell him what had happened. I didn't want him to find out from other people or through social media. He took the news very hard.

And now, I felt numbness again. *What's really going on, God?* I wondered. *What has happened here? How did it get this far? How did our family get so broken, so destroyed?* I really could feel the anguish of Job at this point. I could understand exactly how he must have felt to come out and hear his servants tell him he had lost his children and his livestock … then have his wife come against him, to telling him to curse God and die. I wanted to say, "God, I trust You." But at this point, I was just lost, hurt, and more than anything, afraid.

I'm always having to be strong for everybody. When is someone going to be there for me, God? Where are You? I wondered. I was mentally drained and couldn't find any solace anywhere. But I knew I couldn't go back to substance abuse or any other sinful behavior that would just leave me empty.

I remember sitting on the bathroom floor one night thinking, *God, How do I act? What do I do?*

This can go either way. I can say, "This is not my responsibility. I don't want to deal with this, because he left me." Or I can stand up and be what You called me to be. What is it that You want me to do in this? Whatever it is, I will need Your strength. I can't do this on my own. I can't do this because nobody really knows the real truth. Few even knew Steve and I were separated. I didn't publicize it; there weren't a lot of people who knew other than close family and close friends.

Now my flesh was saying; *To hell with it! You don't have to do anything. It's not your responsibility. You've got to figure out how to keep a roof over your head and how to take care of your son. This man had been gone away from you for a year. But of course my love for Steve...* was entirely too deep to not do what I needed to do as his wife; rather we had been estranged from each other for one year or many years. It didn't matter how things had gone between us in the past; I simply wanted to do what was right in a peaceful and respectable way for him and our children. I also knew that God allowed this to happen for a reason; and although it was painful right at the moment, I knew the Lord would reveal it to me.

God also reminded me, "You know, there have been many times that you've left Me. But every time you left Me, I've always been right there when you turned back to Me. I've never left you, I've never forsaken you. And in this, I'm not going to forsake you. I want you keep doing what you're doing. When you do it, you will find out things that *could* cause you to lose spiritual ground and pull you back to what you've been able to overcome so far. But I will be with you."

As God began to speak to me, I knew He was getting ready to take me through another transition. "This is going to be something far deeper than all the other challenges I have allowed you to go through," He said. "I'm going to develop something in you."

When you have been so soul-tied to a person for many years, then all of a sudden they're not there anymore, you look back and wonder what you could have done or said differently. At the funeral, I thought back to that day Steve and I sat in the attorney's office a week prior to him dying. I remembered seeing his face and knowing that despite everything, he really had not wanted things to get to this point. But I knew there was nothing left within me. *God, how did this end this way?* I wondered. I didn't really know what to do from there.

I faced yet another test of my faith: I didn't really know what to do from there. Here I was, left with all of the responsibility of the debt that we had together. I'd been left trying to figure out how to be a good stepmother to Kedric and Terrance and how to be a mother to Dion, who was in a serious legal situation whose outcome had not yet been determined.

After the funeral, we struggled as a family for many days; trying to pull the pieces together, trying to understand how to move on without Steve. The children were hurting, I was hurting, the family was hurting; although we are a strong family, this was a very difficult time for everyone. And yet I was still dealing with financial issue regarding the foreclosure of our home, attorney fees, and now funeral expense and other debt.

Just as I was at the point of giving up and packing boxes, I got a phone call from a woman at the Veterans Administration, through which Steve and I had gotten our home loan. "We have been looking at your modification application, and we see that it has been denied several times," she said. "We believe we can help you." After several months, the loan modification was approved.

That was the glimpse of hope I needed! Now I realized that God was not going to remove shelter from me. If He was going to help me through this, surely He would help me over the next hurdle.

"God, I don't know what's going to happen in this, but I trust You," I said. "I know I failed, but I know I trust You. I know there is something You are going to show me in this." I felt revived again.

God also blessed me to be able to pay for the funeral expenses ... after I passed a test within the test. Now here is where I have to emphasize; it's so important to listen for God's voice. Sometimes it's hard when you have so many people in your ears and you're so distraught, you don't know which way to go, you don't know what to follow. Sometimes God allows us to stay in the valley so that we're silent and will hear Him. In the Old Testament, David had his cave-Adullam experience. God had to deal with David, who was on the run from King Saul, had lost everything, and had nowhere to turn (1 Samuel 22; Psalms 57, 142). We think of caves as bad places, but sometimes, it's places like these where we can best hear God.

"God, You haven't forgotten me," I said. "You've showed me a glimpse of hope." He'd showed me how He can make a way out of no way. All I had to do is trust Him, believe He is God … and obey. I love what Proverbs 21:1 says: "The king's heart is in the hand of the LORD, as the rivers of water: he turneth it whithersoever he will." God has a way of turning the heart of those in authority over us and those whose influence can benefit us. He will cause these people to change their rules and their policies in our favor.

Now, my faith having gotten that big boost, I was really excited. "If you did that for me, God, I *know* I believe You to take care of this situation with Dion," I said.

On the advice of the attorney, Dion took a plea deal, which meant immediate incarceration. Walking away from my son that day in court was the hardest thing I've *ever* had to do.

But I know we go through things for a reason. God showed me one day in prayer that Dion's anger had been escalating to the point that had he not been stopped at the time he was, he would have made a decision that would have taken his life. Sometimes, what we *think* is a bad situation is really God's way of protecting and preserving us.

And since Dion's incarceration, I've seen him develop into the man I knew he could be. I believe God is using Dion's prison stay for His benefit. He's using me to minister to my son in a way I never thought I would have to do, through prison bars. Not only do I have his ear now; his heart is open to what I have to say. So do I think the answer to Dion's healing was prison? No. I believe the answer to his prison was healing!

I won't share Dion's entire story; I'll let him do that in his own book. But God showed me that prison is, in fact, Dion's training ground for ministry. Nobody wants such difficult training ground; everybody wants the easy road. I admit I would rather my son be right there with me on Sunday morning, preaching. But not everybody's ministry is like that. Not everybody ministers from the pulpit. Dion's training ground may be in a different place, but it's the same training. He's ministering to other people as I'm feeding him. God is preparing him for something so much greater. He's preparing me, too. Prison ministry is not something I thought I would find myself attached to. But now I find myself researching the system because God has turned my heart toward it.

"You thought the miracle you wanted to see was on the front end, but I'm going to give you the miracle on the back end," God told me. "When I get through taking you through this process, both of you will know that it was nobody but Me who brought you through."

And after all, some of the Bible's most prominent men of the faith were in prison. Joseph wouldn't have chosen prison. The Apostle Paul wouldn't have chosen prison. Who would choose that route? Joseph saw in a dream what he would become. He knew what God called him to do, but he didn't understand it. And he went and shared his dream with the wrong people. His own family didn't understand the anointing that was on his life. He didn't think he'd have to spend 13 years as a slave and a prison inmate.

Sometimes we have to go through different experiences in life things before we end up where God really wants us to be. Going through the process isn't always easy or quick. But with God, we *will* get through it.

Father God, help us as parents not to allow our problems and issues to destroy the children that You have placed in our care. Help us to properly nurture them now, so that we won't find ourselves frantically trying to pull them out of serious trouble later. Please help us resist the temptation to hide our sins rather than confessing and repenting, especially when those sins have the power to adversely affect our children. Also, Lord, please help us to simply trust You to fight our battles. Help us to realize, however, that Your blessings don't always come in the manner we expect but are blessings nonetheless; and that out of the worst, most unthinkable scenarios that can occur in our lives, You can bring the most good. In the name of Jesus our Lord, Amen.

Chapter Ten

YOU Still Win!

As my story has shown, battles will spring up the life of every believer. Tribulation is no respecter of persons. Just because you became a believer does not mean you will have an easy life. Not one of us is exempt from trouble, hardship, disappointment, loss. However, victory is assured for the believer!

As a believer, your victory comes from your knowledge of, and confidence in, God and His Word ... and your reliance on the Holy Spirit when you are engaged in battle. His responsibility at this time is to lead and guide you. The leadership of the Holy Spirit, and the specific instructions He gives us concerning the battles we are facing, will cause us to be triumphant.

Along with battles, you will face afflictions. Vocabulary.com defines "affliction" as "a cause of great suffering and distress" and "a state of great suffering and distress due to adversity." You're not the first and you won't be the last to experience suffering and distress.

But know that:

God will comfort those who are afflicted through His Word.

"This is my comfort in my affliction: for thy word hath quickened me." (Psalm 119:50).

God will chose you for a great work right in the midst of your affliction.

"Behold, I have refined thee, but not with silver; I have chosen thee in the furnace of affliction." (Isaiah 48:10).

Those who have not the Word are offended when affliction arises.

"And [they] have no root in themselves, and so endure but for a time: afterward, when affliction or persecution ariseth for the word's sake, immediately they are offended." (Mark 4:17).

Those who are suffering affliction must pray.

"Is any among you afflicted? let him pray." (James 5:13a).

Our faith is how we conquer battles in our life (sickness, poverty, bondage, and pressure).

"For whatsoever is born of God overcometh the world: and this is the victory that overcometh the world, even our faith." (1 John 5:4).

Let's talk about that word "faith," which is defined in Hebrews 11:1 as "the substance of things hoped for, the evidence of things not seen." We need faith to realize victorious results when we face battles and afflictions. Faith is a practical expression of the confidence you have in God and His Word. Remember: Every attack you face in life is an attack on your faithfulness! You will not have to endure anything God has not already empowered you to go through.

"But why must I face the battles anyway, if God is going to fight them for me?" you might ask. My question to you is, How will you develop, spiritually and otherwise, if you don't have battles to win?

Psalm 27:14 tells us, "Wait on the LORD: be of good courage, and he shall strengthen thine heart: wait, I say, on the LORD." God did not make losers, therefore we are not to think, or speak, defeat. As a matter of fact, when you are facing what looks to be a formidable battle, *you must declare yourself the winner before the battle begins.* This is what it means to speak things into existence, as referred to in Romans 4:17: "(As it is written, I have made thee a father of many nations,) before him whom he believed, [even] God, who quickeneth the dead, and calleth those things which be not as though they were."

Although speaking victory is key, you can't just speak. You have to *study* to be able to stand on the Word.

We are victorious based on our knowledge of God; therefore, our victory is obtained through spending time in the Word of God. The Word provides spiritual strength, just like food provides strength for your physical body. As knowledge produces strength, strength produces victory. What you have on the inside of you will determine the degree of victory you experience in your life. Conversely, a lack of the Word inside you will determine your defeat. When you don't rely on the Word, you make bad decisions.

Consider 2 Cor. 2:14: "Now thanks be unto God, which always causeth us to triumph in Christ, and maketh manifest the savour of his knowledge by us in every place." Knowing that God will always cause us to triumph, we can walk in holy confidence. Also consider Hebrews 10:32: "But call to remembrance the former days, in which, after ye were illuminated, ye endured a great fight of afflictions." Confidence is a key to victory! You must know who you are in Christ. As your confidence rises, you can assume an offensive position against the enemy.

Again, know that the victory that overcomes the world is your faith. Enter the battle from a position of victory, with confidence in God's ability to bring you out as the winner. You will WIN if we allow the anointing of God to lead you through the paths of darkness. In the time of trouble, He will sustain you when your mind is on Him! You need only "fight the good fight of faith" (1 Timothy 6:12).

What weapons, besides your faith, prayer, and the Word, will you use in your battle?

As I've already indicated, you need the Holy Spirit. As Jesus told the Apostles in Acts 1:8: "Ye shall receive power, after that the Holy Ghost is come upon you." You will not be able to win without Him.

Thanksgiving can be used as a weapon; it expands our capacity to receive.

"Now thanks be unto God, which always causeth us to triumph in Christ, and maketh manifest the savour of his knowledge by us in every place" (2 Corinthians 2:14).

Another weapon is our anointing. Our victory is only guaranteed in Christ, the Anointed One, and His anointing. Burdens are removed and yokes are destroyed because of the anointing. To "anoint" means to rub on or rub into. God is rubbing His wisdom on us.

Yes, the anointing will cost you — you must pay the price of prayer and another weapon of warfare: Praise. Look at how Judah, led by Jehoshaphat, was able to whip its enemies in 2 Chron. 20:20-22:

> **And they rose early in the morning, and went forth into the wilderness of Tekoa: and as they went forth, Jehoshaphat stood and said, Hear me, O Judah, and ye inhabitants of Jerusalem; Believe in the LORD your God, so shall ye be established; believe his prophets, so shall ye prosper.**

And when he had consulted with the people, he appointed singers unto the LORD, and that should praise the beauty of holiness, as they went out before the army, and to say, Praise the LORD; for his mercy endureth forever.

And when they began to sing and to praise, the LORD set ambushments against the children of Ammon, Moab, and mount Seir, which were come against Judah; and they were smitten.

The Lord God is described in Psalm 24:8 as "mighty in battle." And praise is essential when it comes to your battle!

Holiness, mentioned in the passage above, is another weapon. Heaven is calling on us to go to a higher level of holiness, which, essentially, is being of one mind with God. 1 Peter 1:16 gives us a reminder of what was clearly stated in the Old Testament: "Because it is written, Be ye holy; for I am holy."

Yet another weapon is wisdom. Wisdom is the ability to know what to do in the spirit when in the flesh, you don't know what to do. The spirit of wisdom and understanding, the spirit of counsel and might, the spirit of knowledge, and the fear of the Lord reside in us. People were so impressed by Jesus' wisdom and His mighty works that they wondered about the source of His power: "And when he was come into his own country, he taught them in their synagogue, insomuch that they were astonished, and said, Whence hath this man this wisdom, and these mighty works?" (Matthew 13:54).

Now that you know the tools to win your battles, here is your 10-step battle plan to ensure victory.

1. **Believe the Bible.** Believe that the bible is REAL and that God's anointing rests upon every word.

2. **Read and study the Word.** You can't rely on the Word without knowing it. Become intimate with the WORD OF GOD.

3. **Renew your mind with the Word.** Allow it to change your thinking about your situation. Saturate your mind with God's thoughts, found in His Word, instead of the problem you see in front of you. "For we walk by faith, not by sight." (2 Cor. 5:7)

4. **Honor the Word by making it the final authority in your life.** Part of your faith walk involves faith that God's Word is bigger than your problem!

5. **Set your mind on victory.** Speak VICTORY over your situation! Declare yourself as the winner.

6. **Obey the Word.** Do not go back to what is familiar! Follow through on the plan of God.

7. **Use your mouth as a weapon to launch covenant talks.** Continue to PROCLAIM the Word, and not your problem.

8. **Labor to enter into rest.** Refuse to worry. Have peace. Keep your mind on the Word.

9. **Never forget to pray.** Every failure in life is a prayer failure. Commune with God; stir up the spirit of might.

10. **Don't quit.** Be consistent and remain patient. Don't give up in the middle of the battle.

Most importantly, remember that Jesus died for ALL our sins; therefore, no situation is so bad, raunchy, pitiful, degrading, embarrassing or tragic that you can't have victory over it with God's help. You can still win!

We love You, Lord. We worship You and Praise Your Holy name. And we thank You for all our blessings. We thank You for your willingness to deliver us from our pits of destruction and our miry clay. We thank you in advance for victory over any problem, and in any battle, we know that whatever we ask You for, it's "already done." And we thank You most of all for your Son, whose death was followed by His resurrection and resulted in a happy ending for us. In His name, by which we pour out our supplications, we also pour out our adoration. Amen.

EPILOGUE

I've come out of my process having learned so much about what marriage is and what it isn't. And now I know I'm more precious than rubies and that there are certain things I shouldn't and don't have to allow, just in a bid to keep someone. Even before I got pregnant with Dion, there were incidents during my marriage to Steve that made me wonder whether I should go home to my mom. But I thought I needed to stick it out, as did others in my family who found themselves in unhappy marriages. I didn't want to be divorced because of what people would say or think. I went through many, many things to be where I am today. Now I'm reaping the benefits of the favor God, including favor with one of His sons.

One evening, sometime after Steve had left, I was sitting there at my second job, which was at a hotel. A gentleman was walking through the office. He paused near the front desk, where I was working.

"A beautiful woman like you should not look so down and depressed," he said in a pleasant tone.

"You need to smile. I think that'll make your day better."

I didn't even look up.

A short time later, I get flowers at the job. I thought at first that they were from Steve. I thought maybe his conscience was bothering him about walking away and leaving me with so many problems ... and that this was his way of apologizing.

The note on the card simply said, *From someone who loves to see you smile.*

I didn't know who it was. But I thought, *God, there has got to be a ray of hope in this situation. I've got to find my way out of this. If I look this down to this person, God, how do I look to You? I know that if You're in me, there's no reason I should be this way. I've got to see myself through this. I've got to figure out how You're going to lead me out of this because I know what Your Word says ... I know You're not going to leave me here to just die like this.*

The flowers continued, along with cards and notes bearing such messages as "I've been admiring you ... I'm beginning to see the smile on your face ... When I come through town all I want to do is see the smile on your face." *OK, God,* I thought. *I don't know who this is, but help me not to read too much into this. If it's just someone You've sent my way only to encourage me, help me to realize it.*

My admirer, Ernest, eventually revealed himself. He lived out of state, but came to town for business periodically. We began a good, wholesome friendship that blossomed into a wholesome, Godly romance.

Hearing Ernest's testimony about what God brought him to, and brought him *through*, caused me to start finding myself again. I now understood that God doesn't allow us to go through valleys to forget whom He is, but rather to remember that He's the one who brings us through our pain. I just had to press through all the darkness — and remember who God was.

One would think I wouldn't *want* another man in my life. Many women feel this way after being mistreated and abandoned by men. I told God I didn't want to be a lonely, bitter woman for the rest of my life. I've seen women like this, in and out of church; when a good man does come along, they miss out because they are guarding their hearts too closely. I asked God to condition my heart to where I could love again. "God, I desire to have someone in my life who loves me for whom I am and whom You created me to be," I prayed.

Sometimes we think there's no longer any hope or we're too old and we might as well be by ourselves. But that didn't happen with me. Despite the outcome of my first marriage, I loved *being a wife*. God knew what my heart desired ... and he certainly sent my

Boaz. Women who are familiar with the book of Ruth in the Bible say they want a Boaz, but don't think about the fact that Ruth would not have gotten to her Boaz had she not lost her first husband, left all she knew to go into a strange land, and remained devoted to her mother-in-law. I tell women all the time, "You're talking about Boaz; do you know who Ruth really was?"

I'm glad to have triumphed over serious challenges, as Ruth had to do, and to be able to go into the next chapter of my life with a man that I know loves me. At the time I wrote this book, Ernest and I were preparing for marriage. We took our time with courtship. I love courtship and I don't think people understand the importance of it. Courting one another, getting to know one another, is wonderful. And Ernest befriended and courted me for a long time before I decided he was the one God sent. He has seen some of the tragedy I've gone through, been a good listener and a good friend, and never imposed upon me in a way that made me feel uncomfortable. He has been very patient, very kind, and has demonstrated wisdom. It's important to have someone you know that can weather a storm for you. He has shown himself to be able to weather that storm. He's been there through some bad times with me, Dion's ordeal and all. We're looking forward to the good times.

BIBLIOGRAPHY

Affliction [Def. 1]. (n). In Vocabulary.com. Retrieved July 31, 2015, from http://www.vocabulary.com/dictionary/affliction.

Gotquestions.org. http://www.gotquestions.org/soul-spirit.html. "What is the difference between the soul and spirit of man?"

Holmes, Leonard. "When Grief Gets Complicated," About.com. http://mentalhealth.about.com/od/griefandmourning/a/compgrief.htm. Updated June 8, 2015.

Mental [Def. 1]. (adj.). Aol.com. Retrieved July 31, 2015, from

http://search.aol.com/aol/search?s_it=topsearchbox.search&v_t=keyword_rollover&q=mental+definition.

Morrow, Angela. "Grief and Mourning: What's Normal and What's Not?: Normal Grief and Complicated Grief," About.com. http://dying.about.com/od/thegrievingprocess/a/griefprocess.htm. Updated Dec. 16, 2014.

Shear, Katherine; Ellen Frank, Patricia R. Houck, and Charles F. Reynolds. "Treatment of Complicated Grief: A Randomized Controlled Trial." JAMA. 293, (June 2005): pp. 2601-2608.

Spiritual [Def. 1]. (adj.). In Aol.com. Retrieved July 31, 2015, from http://search.aol.com/aol/search?s_it=topsearchbox.search&v_t=keyword_rollover&q=spiritual+definition.

Tims, Riva. When it All Falls Apart: Find Healing, Joy and Victory through the Pain. Lake Mary, Fla.: Charisma House. March 6, 2012.

All Scripture references are taken from the Holy Bible, King James Version (KJV), first published 1611.

ABOUT THE AUTHOR

Pastor Tiffany Robinson is one of the most transparent vessels in the Kingdom of God today. She is known as a "game changer" because of her kingdom perspective regarding moving on the voice of God despite traditional barriers. With more than 10 years of ministerial experience, Pastor Robinson serves as the Senior Pastor of Changed Life International Ministries in North Little Rock, AR. She is one of the most sought-after ministers for women's conferences as she speaks to the souls of listeners, sharing with them about the adversities she has overcome through the power of God.

Winners Never Quit and Quitters Never Win!

The authority of the believer comes in understanding that in every Attack and every Affliction, YOU STILL WIN!

Now thanks be unto God, which always causeth us to triumph in Christ, and maketh manifest the savour of his knowledge by us in every place.

— 2 Corinthian 2:14 KJV